Table of Contents

Introduction 5
Why Build A Cult? 7
But "Politics?" 8
What Is a Cult? 9
Types of Cults 10
    Famous Crash-And-Burn Cults 10
    Controversial Cults 10
    Small Group Cult 11
    The Invisible Cult 11
The Mind Of The Cult Leader 13
Self Acceptance 14
For Greater Self Acceptance 18
The Plan 19
How To Find Out What You Want..21
Patience 22
Rational Objectivity 22
Strengthening Your Rational Objectivity..................................23
Ways To Control Emotions...24
Obsession 24
Ways For Balancing Thoughts, Feelings, And Actions....................25
Your Life as A Saga 26
The Cult Organization 32
Cult Purpose 32
Cult Mythos 33
Processes That Maintain The Cult Structure 35
Cult Values 37
Cult Doctrine 38
Cult Structure and Cult Culture 40
The Line Of Command 40
Cult Values And The Line of Command 42
Creating a Group Bond..42

www.BuildingYourCult.com

Building Your Cult

Elitism 44
Special Mission, Purpose or Destiny 44
Make It Difficult To Join..45
Create Initiations 46
Secret Knowledge Only Insiders Know 46
Create Mysterious And Unprovable Rumors 46
Membership And The Individual's Personal Saga 47
Commitment And Consistency 48
Human Resources And Man Management 49
Recruiting 50
Indoctrination 51
Acceptance 52
Challenge 53
The Non-Disclosure Agreement (NDA) 53
Reinforcement 54
Reminding Each Member Of Their Importance 54
Ask For Sacrifice 54
Reward Them And Keep Their Bellies Full 55
Removal 56
Advanced HR Training 57
The Motivational Imperative..57
 Doctrine 59
The Doctrine Of This Book 60
The One Person 60
The Two Promises To Remember 61
The Promise To Remember That You Are Loved 61
The Promise To Remember Your Greater Destiny 63
The Three Internal Forces..64
Thinking 65
Feeling 65
Doing 66
Awareness of Thoughts, Feelings and Actions 67
The Many 68
Uniting The Many 68

www.BuildingYourCult.com

Building Your Cult

by
Dantalion Jones
Author of the books

Mind Control Language Patterns

Perfected Mind Control:
The Unauthorized Black Book of Hypnotic Mind Control

Cult Control

The Handbook Of Psychic Cold Reading

Mind Control Hypnosis

Mind Control 101: How To Influence The Thoughts And Actions of Others Without Them Knowing and Caring

The Full Fact Book Of Seduction Patterns:
The Cocky & Funny Edition

All These Books Available Online Bookstores

Other Products by Dantalion Jones:

The Delta Success Program

The Handbook of Psychic Cold Reading

Building Your Cult

Copyright Dantalion Jones 2010

ISBN - 1450590837
EAN -13 – 9781450590839

All rights reserved. Without limiting the rights under copyrights reserved above, no part of this publication may be reproduced, stored in, or introduced into a retrieval system, or transmitted, in any form or by any means (electronic, mechanical, photocopying, recording, or otherwise), without the prior written permission of the copyright owner.

Dedication

To my faithful djinn, familiar and constant companion, Dantalion, the 71st spirit of the Goetia, "His Office is to teach all Arts and Sciences unto any; and to declare the Secret Counsel of any one; for he knoweth the Thoughts of all Men and Women, and can change them at his Will. He can cause Love, and show the Similitude of any person, and show the same by a Vision, let them be in what part of the World they Will."

Building Your Cult

Destiny 69
The Trinity of Suffering..70
Fear...70
Pride..71
Ignorance...71
The World 73
Propaganda 73
Personal Propaganda And Image 74
Other Forms Of Personal Propaganda 76
Live Efficiently 78
Fulfilling Peoples Needs...79
The 5 Cental Human Needs..79
The Seven Relationship Needs...82
Creating The Organization To Fulfill Your Ambitions 84
Recap Of Doctrine 85
Build Your Own Personal Doctrine 86
Last Piece of Advice: Learn Hypnosis...86
A Story..88
Unleash the Addict 91
    What is "Unleash The Addict"?..93
    Why Teach "Unleash The Addict"? 93
    I Am Not The Information Police..93
    People Want To Know If This Is Possible 94
    People Want To Know How To Do It 94
    People Want To Know How To Undo An Addiction 94
    People Want To Protect Themselves From Manipulation 95
    People Want To Be Able To Do This To Themselves...................95
    People Want To Coach Others For Fitness Addiction...................95
    People Want To Do It To Other People 95
    My Understanding Of Addictions..96
Confidence..98
Getting Into People's Minds And The Need For Rapport................100
Ways To Build Rapport..100
Pacing And Dragging...102

www.BuildingYourCult.com

Building Your Cult

The Two Types Of Pull..103
The Compelling Pull...103
Statement Of Responsible Use...107
Qualifying Your Subject...109
The Addictive Pull...110
Anchoring..112
Eliciting The State 112
Setting The Anchor..113
Testing The Anchor...113
Firing The Anchor...113
Putting It All Together...113
The Propulsion System..114
Final Words..119

Building Your Cult

Introduction

This book deals with the art and science of protecting and promoting your own interests. It is about reaching that pinnacle of accomplishment where you have groups of people devoted to you, your goals and your ambitions. In other words, it is about the politics of life.

It is about making your own cult.

No one has to build a cult from this book. That's a personal decision and you'll get some very useful tools to do that... if you decide.

What this book should do is help you to create a personal sense of purpose.

More often when someone talks about a sense of purpose or a feeling of destiny they are met with cynicism. People generally don't even have a language to understand the concept of purpose and destiny.

Yes, we have plans and goals and problems to solve and we work to solve those problems but there are few who can say they are driven by a sense of purpose. Those who are are usually are live like unstoppable forces of nature.

If you have to wait to find your sense of purpose then it will likely never happen. Right NOW you are in the perfect place to choose your purpose. When you do, life gains a clearer perspective and you can do the ordinary and mundane acts of daily life with more vigor and joy because everything is connected by your sense of purpose.

If you decide to build a cult, good luck. I simply ask that you use your sense of purpose to be one of the smart cult leaders and do good works that make people better than when you first met them.

The world of cults can be divided into four different kinds. The first you've all heard about because they burn out in a blaze of glory – Waco, Heaven's Gates, and Peoples Temple will immediately

Building Your Cult

come to mind.

The second type of cult is swirling with controversy and stigma: Scientology, Jehovah's Witnesses, and Hare Krishnas.

The third type of cult is usually small and unheard of. They form in small groups and homes for prayer vigils, psychic surgeries and space alien rendezvous.

But a fourth type of cult you would never recognize because they do nothing strange enough to be seen as out of the ordinary, yet their followers are devout, even fanatical. Their leaders would never be considered cult leaders. In fact, they may be unknown to many of their followers, yet these leaders revel in the opulence they've created in their own lives by having such a devout following. This will be referred to as "The Invisible Cult" and by far is the best and most preferred way to organize people. As the leader of the Invisible Cult you will enjoy more benefits and fewer problems than any other cult.

The goal of this book is to introduce you to the methods and mindset of this type of cult and the leader behind it.

Within this book you will experience what it is like inside the mind of someone with untouchable power, and decide whether or not you want it for yourself.

This book is divided into two parts. The first part explores the mind of the cult leader and offers a few exercises that will help develop your own set of cult leader insights. It is here that you will uncover an untapped wealth spring of power that we all control. The second part of the book is about the management of your cult from the microcosm of the individual recruit to its larger organizational structure, all the way to dealing with the world outside the cult. You will be given enough information to decide if this is a realm of power you want to exploit for yourself, or if it's enough to be merely entertained learning about it.

Building Your Cult

Why Build A Cult?

Years ago my very first book was written: "Cult Control." Today I look back on it as an early effort, but it was a start. Since then I have written many books on mind control, NLP, hypnosis, mind reading and self improvement.

Each one of the books followed a theme about how the mind works, but there is a deeper theme that runs throughout all of the madness ... power and control. All of my work eventually led me to another level, the level of politics.

Because of that first book, many people contact me seeking assistance starting their own cult. To my knowledge none of them have had much success. What I learned, however, was that my instruction had been lacking.

I was not clear enough on specifically what they have to do with themselves and how they need to act within the world. What they needed to do was first deeply focus on why they wanted a cult, and then work on building the interpersonal and political skills necessary in order to gain the power.

What we are to learn is that everything is a vie for power in this world where we all have to interact with others. To avoid or deny that fact would only make us more vulnerable.

Forming a cult is the ultimate petri dish for political experimentation. Of course, considerable time and energy must be invested in the endeavor, but the potential rewards can be staggering. Among the benefits:

- Having a dedicated and loyal people working with you to help you achieve your goals
- Commanding a group of people who share your values
- The power to creatively experiment in whatever direction interests you
- Money, and lots of it

www.BuildingYourCult.com

Building Your Cult

- Social connections
- The admiration and worship of others
- Power

There are countless examples of how people in cults have been exploited by their leaders, so no need to discuss that topic here. There are enough ways to prosper and develop your own cult that doesn't involve abusing and hurting people. Growing your own cult is a way to create your own society from the ground up. You'll discover that those cults which treat their followers with a degree of respect ultimately gain the most power and cash in the end.

But "Politics?"

Politics is the art of promoting and protecting your own interests. Anyone who says they don't play politics is either lying, living isolated from others or dead. The reason that I'm turning a microscope to the realm of politics is that if you are to deal with people you must recognize the role that politics plays. Building a successful cult can bring you to the pinnacle of political power, but note, this book doesn't tell you to form a cult. It only reveals how.

There are several ways you can respond to this information.

- You can take the idea of building a cult seriously, unleash your desire for power, and set to making it a reality.
- You can learn the mindset of a cult leader without building a cult and thereby make your life more effective.
- You can read it, find it interesting, put it down and go on with your life as it was before picking this book up.

The choice is yours. At the very least I hope you take the second option. Allow me to explain why.

Several years ago I wrote **The Forbidden Book Of Getting What You Want** as my personal vision of what a self-help book

Building Your Cult

should be about. It remains my absolute favorite. When people ask me which of my books I would recommend it is always at the top of the list. It came to me like divine inspiration. However, in spite of its quality it's my other books on mind control that people seem to want the most.

My solution was to write a book that appealed to the base and prurient desires in people and hide my self improvement message somewhere inside it. If you want to build a cult efficiently then it will be essential to do some work on yourself. Whether you build a cult or not is up to you. If you go through the processes in this book (not just read them) you'll gain some insights about yourself that will help you expand your power in the world. Ultimately, you should be a better and happier person whether or not you make an attempt at cult building.

What Is a Cult?

First let's take the word "cult" and neutralize it. The word "cult" simply is a short variant of the word "culture," but meant to describe a smaller group of people with a set of beliefs that is different from the culture at large. The word "cult" is used indiscriminately in the media to refer to any group with seemingly bizarre beliefs and rituals. The reason people respond so adversely to the word is because of another word – "exploitation." People don't like to think that they exploit other people…but everyone does this daily through the use of their skills, talents and abilities. Functionally the words "use" and "exploit" mean the same thing. Anything that does not server us in some way we will eventually toss aside. This is true of people as well; a friend who does not provide what friends give quickly looses the status of "friend".

Your invisible cult may be a small business where you want your employees to be loyal and dedicated to you and your product or service. Your invisible cult may be a subscriber list of those who you want to value your information. Your cult may be a spiritual

Building Your Cult

following who you want to be eager to give and volunteer to your cause. Your invisible cult could simply be those friends you most value. For those who are a part of your invisible cult you will find, if done well, none of them will feel manipulated or exploited.

Within all of the many "cults" that people are involved in they fight for their own interests within the group. Politics will play a key roll in your success. Many of your choices and decisions will determine the success of your cult.

Types of Cults

A cult will develop into one of four types depending on the actions and choices of the cult leaders.

Famous Crash-And-Burn Cults

The Crash-and-Burn cult is famous because they are the ones that make the news and that people remember the most.

Ask just someone to name a cult and a short list will come to mind: Jonestown, Heaven's Gate, David Koresh and Branch Davidians, The Charles Manson Family.

These cults share several things in common. Firstly, they became famous because people died. Secondly, their leaders became so self absorbed and delusional the their decisions were not connected to reality. This disconnection progressed until they perceived themselves to be able to break laws without consequences.

It goes without saying that to fall in this first category of cult would not bode well for the success of you or your cult. We'll later discuss some good strategies that will help you succeed without becoming delusional with power.

Controversial Cults

The controversial cult is so named because, like the Crash-and-Burn cult, it is likely to be in the news but without the tendency

Building Your Cult

towards suicide. Their controversy comes from the numbers of people that lay in waste when the cult no longer finds them useful. Some of these types of cults also gain controversy by how viciously they attack their former cult members, and often resort to lawsuits, hazing, and other forms of semi-legal harassment.

Small Group Cult

The small group cult differs from the controversial cult only in its size. Because it is smaller it becomes easier for certain abuses to to slip under the radar of the media.

Smaller cults may lack certain essentials necessary to maintain a working infrastructure, and as a result can die out quickly. The upside of being small is that they can easily make rapid changes to any aspect of the group. A cult leader may start with a spiritual/religious cult but, finding it unprofitable, can add to it the multi-level marketing of nutritional supplements. If that prospers then the leader can focus solely on the MLM cult.

The Invisible Cult

Just as the name implies, the Invisible Cult is either unseen or unrecognized as a cult yet it incorporates many of the aspects engendered by other cults: loyalty, an elitist attitude, a brotherly bond among it's followers. It is the Invisible Cult that this book wants you to focus on.

Invisible Cults tend to be efficient because they balance the exploitation of its followers with keeping them happy and satisfied – not a simple task. By maintaining happy and compliant followers they avoid the scrutiny of media and contribute to the world while its leadership silently prospers.

Numerous fraternal groups are organized to act as Invisible cults by *discouraging* new members, and thus adding to their mystique and their appeal. Those who do join will fit a model of what a fraternity brother should be, and are rewarded with privileges

Building Your Cult

as members.

Another example of an Invisible Cult is Harley Davidson motorcycles. Harley Davidson creates a quality motorcycle and offers it with an elitist attitude. Those who own a Harley Davidson motorcycle and those who build them feel they are a special group of individuals separate from the normal pack of humanity and separate from other motorcycle owners. Consider the community and cultural ties that Harley Davidson owners share. Do you know the names of the individuals owners who benefit the most from the Harley Davidson culture? I don't but I can assure you it's the upper management and stock holders of the Harley Davidson company.

So it is that YOU can build your own cult, an invisible cult, that makes other feel happy, special, fulfilled, and that allows you to prosper. Soon you'll learn the great secrets of politics and man management that can make your cult both successful and invisible.

Building Your Cult

The Mind Of The Cult Leader

If you are to have a cult that is different from other cults – successful, prosperous and free from scrutiny – then you must plan to be different from other cult leaders and from other people. This difference should be enough that it sets you apart, but not so much that it alienates you from others.

You may find that the life of a cult leader can be one of drastic dichotomy. On the one hand you will be surrounded by peers, subordinates and sycophants, but it can be a very lonely life in that you will find very few people you can trust who also understand your vision and share your ambition.

To avoid this loneliness it is a good idea to remind yourself that by helping others with their goals and ambitions they can be helping you. It is politics, after all. By learning the goals and ambitions of others you connect with your fellow humans while building your resources. You'll find that by giving people encouragement where they want it they will likely do the same for you. It will also help forestall the type of isolation that causes other cult leaders to spiral down into paranoid megalomania.

Involve yourself in the politics of life, unlike the crash-and-burn cult leaders who separate themselves with their fear and paranoia. But this too can be hard, for you will be subjected to all the envies and petty power plays suffered by anyone in power. You must learn to be calm and detached enough that you can see the world and your mission in it clearly.

In this section you will get into the mind of the ideal invisible cult leader and see how he or she thinks and acts. You'll be given exercises that will build the mental strength you will need in this most political world. You will develop a strength and certainty about who you are, and then you will go into motion by focusing on a mission, a destiny and purpose that will be both the polar star that guides your actions and the powerful engine that propels you there.

Building Your Cult

At this point is it good to remember the words of China's historic general and author of **The Art Of War**, Sun Tsu. "Being unconquerable lies with yourself."

Choosing to become a cult leader (make that a good and effective cult leader) requires more responsibility than you might imagine. It means being responsible for your emotional reactions. While there are many people who have attempted controlling others through a cult, there are very few who have truly mastered control over their own emotions. Those who possess power over their emotions are like forces of nature, like a fierce, unyielding wind to the desert sands. This is because they have mastered the ability to remain calm and detached so they can move and react without the cloud of emotions distracting them.

Self Acceptance

Self acceptance is the first quality of the invisible cult leader we will examine. It may at first seem to be a strange place to start. However, it is vital for success, and, on the other hand, can create volatility if misunderstood or taken to the wrong extreme.

The culture at large tends to enforce a sense of self loathing in people. Jewish guilt and Christian shame live as examples of the evils of a righteous life. What you will find within the personalities of a truly effective cult leaders is just the opposite, because inwardly they know they are good and lovable. This is even true if they outwardly preach the gospel of guilt and shame. The only exception to this is when they are caught and exposed committing some act against their gospel or code. They must then publicly repent before they can continue on with their mission.

Many failed crash-and-burn cult leaders seem to have monstrous and narcissistic egos. This extreme of narcissism inevitably leads to their downfall, but it was also is essential for their personal climb to power. The ego and self love (and self acceptance) must be moderated and utilized like a potentially toxic vitamin. The

Building Your Cult

right amount will make and keep you strong, but too much will kill you.

One may fear that building a cult may lead to narcissism and grandiosity so it's important to offer a few pointers how to notice and counter that possibility.

Understand, narcissistic personalities are filled with envy and they display it by 1) bragging and name dropping to build themselves up and 2) belittling and undermining others so that they appear better by comparison. Therefor the first thing you must be aware of within yourself is envy; wanting what other people have or hating them for having it.

You can prevent this envy by making sure you measure yourself *only by your own standard* and no one else'. The standard you set is based upon your unshakable sense of purpose and destiny that you create. You will find that when you compare yourself only to yourself you will always be satisfied.

The next step to counter narcissism can be summed up in two simple words: ***Shut up!***

People with ***real*** power don't brag or belittle because they don't have to. They simply make things happen and let people judge them by their accomplishments. Remember, people who own Lamborghini motor cars don't race them because they know they will beat any other car out there. In ancient Greece the emperor didn't have to give into tirades when someone angered him. All he would have to do is nod his head and man would be executed. Real power does not need to brag or belittle.

Back to acceptance.

Let's make an attempt to understand why self acceptance is so important to success as a truly effective cult leader. For one thing, it's hard to deny that the world is not always kind. There are people out there who not only disagree with you but think of you as the personification of all they hate. There are other people who will keep quiet about their true feelings but will at the same time work to exploit you or find some subtle way to undermine you by sarcasm,

Building Your Cult

name calling, or other subtle expressions of contempt. The worst of these are those closest to you because their actions can have the most damaging affect and can steal the wind from your sails by preoccupying your mind and inflaming your emotions.

While the negative efforts of others cannot be avoided, you should make a strong effort to create the most supportive environment for your goals. The only *true* source of acceptance and love must come from within yourself.

I personally learned this by watching the many people I've worked with as a hypnotist. The reason they would come to me was usually because there was something about themselves that they hated. They were thinking that by hating and rejecting that part of themselves (the part that smoke, the part that ate too much, etc.) they would be able to change. Hating that part of them only made them more miserable, and made that part more resistant to change.

What they learned from working with me is that every part of the individual has a positive intent and means well even if the outcome is bad. The part of a person that over eats is much like a child who want to help you cook but only succeeds at making a mess.

By first loving and accepting that part of themselves they were then able to coax and coerce it to change in a lasting way. The person becomes like a loving parent who recognizes that part's positive intent, but instead of punishing it for the mess it makes it loves it and teaches it what to do better next time.

During the hypnosis session I would describe in detail how they are to henceforth treat themselves:

"Notice now that you can see yourself in the mirror. From this point on when you look in the mirror you LIKE what you see in the mirror. From this point on you LIKE that person you see in the mirror. You LIKE, LOVE and DEEPLY accept yourself, and from this point on you do EVERYTHING in your power to make yourself happy AND HEALTHY. You do everything and MORE because you love

Building Your Cult

yourself."

"Unconscious mind, you like (NAME). You LIKE, LOVE and DEEPLY ACCEPT (NAME), and you do everything and more to make (NAME) happy and healthy. You do EVERYTHING to make (NAME) healthy physically, financially, emotionally and spiritually, and you do EVERYTHING to attract and build the most supportive relationships that lead you to your goals and desires."

"From this point on you release ALL self sabotage. You have no use for it any longer. From this point on you think ONLY of the future. That is THE most important thing to you from this point on."

At times saying these words would bring tears because it was the first time in their lives they were told to treat themselves with love and kindness.

If you wish to better understand this concept of "parts" I highly recommend you read the book Core Transformation by Connirae Andreas. Core Transformation describes how parts are created and gives a process to "unite" them to work with the personality. I highly recommend you learn this process and put yourself through it in order to be aware of the impact it can have.

When you make a concerted effort to love and accept EVERY part of you then these parts in turn begin to be more supportive of your goals as well.

The potential downfall that can come from excesses of self acceptance and love come in the form of narcissistic egotism. When that happens the leader comes to believe that his or her words are the words of God, and should be applied to all people. Under this spell a leader, when depressed, will command his followers into mad exercises of violence or suicide. When

Building Your Cult

in a state of manic self grandeur they cannot grasp how the world would TRULY respond to their ramblings. All you have to do is look at the long list of cult leaders who have predicted the end of the world or, like Charles Mason, have felt that some wild act of violence will start the countdown to "the end of days."

One reason people become cult leaders (and fall into narcissistic egotism) is that it is the only way to find some facsimile of acceptance and love. Charles Manson, as an example, was born to a prostitute and raised in orphanages and prisons. Forming his "Family" in the 1960's gave him a form of acceptance that he lacked in his youth.

To that end it is essential to maintain an objective view of the world and distance yourself from the pitfalls of hubris. You can do this by having people around you who are kind to you but willing to be honest to you.. As an exercise to help you maintain a sense of perspective as you build your invisible cult learn to constantly ask yourself, "how will this action help me accomplish my goal?"

For Greater Self Acceptance

By doing the following exercise will help you begin to connect with that feeling of self acceptance and love. It may seem strange but it has a purpose.

Repeat to yourself with meaning the hypnosis script that I gave you (see above).

It may at first feel strange, but keep doing it until you feel it and believe what you are saying. Also, if you're feeling bad begin singing songs of praise to and about yourself. Include how great you are and how much you love yourself, and call yourself by name as if you are proclaiming your love for another person.

Of course, do NOT do this aloud while anyone is present. You can say it quietly to yourself under your breath if needed and keep a running loop of praise going in your head. It's important to do this when you get up in the morning. You will be surprised how

Building Your Cult

nicely it starts your day.

As mentioned earlier the human psyche can be divided into any number of parts. They are not really different personalities but are more like competing desires and interests. There is the part that wants to eat ice cream, the part that wants you to be healthy, the part that makes you get out of bed in the morning, and the part that convinces you at times to sleep in. Not all of these parts work together towards the same end but they **all** exist to give you **some** form of benefit. It is your duty to unite these parts to serve your and your goals. This next exercise is a meditation to be done with eyes closed in a place of silence.

With your eyes closed do whatever process you need to relax your body and focus your attention on your imagination. You will imagine all the different parts within appearing all at once. Some of them you recognize and appreciate (the part that compels you work out) and some you recognize as less than helpful (the part that wants ice cream at night). All of those parts are to be present and you are to call them forth without condemnation or judgment. Within this scene in your mind you are to create a marriage ceremony that unites all the parts together to help you fulfill your goals and destiny. Within that ceremony give each one of your parts your love (they all mean well, after all) and ask each part to agree to help you on your great mission. The meditation will be complete when you get the feeling that all the parts have agreed. You should feel VERY good when your meditation is complete.

The Plan

The Plan (with a capital "p") is the difference that makes the difference.

Many of us have goals, or at least we say we have goals. The likelihood is that what we call goals are merely vague wishes and hopes of what we would like to happen. These are not plans, and only a fool would delude themselves to think they will have any great impact. It is like planning to retire rich by buying a lottery ticket every week. A plan, on the other hand, is about understanding every step that will lead you to your goal.

Making a Plan of this nature takes thoughtful consideration from beginning to end and includes even how to respond to the inevitable and unpredictable problems that will occur along the way. This is often referred to as "understanding the big picture."

Something happens to the person who takes the time to develop a Plan. They seem to take on an all-knowing sense of calm. This comes from their depth of planning and knowing exactly where everything fits.

The most powerful people in the world will be driven by two aspects of their Plan, what will be referred to as the Outer Plan and the Inner Plan. The Outer Plan has an end result or goal, but the Inner Plan is an open ended process.

The Outer Plan is a real and measurable outcome that can be subject to scrutiny. An Outer Plan is any goal that has a definite ending point. It may be to build a business, or church or ministry. It could be buying a car or building your ideal house. When the Outer Plan is followed a goal is accomplished and another goal, along with it's Outer Plan, can take it's place. You can have many Outer Plans going at a single time with all of them leading to their own conclusion.

The Inner Plan, however, has no end point and it is the driving force that helps you maintain your energy, focus and momentum. Unlike the Outer Plan, The Inner Plan can be kept secret. If you've heard the phrase, "you're only as sick as your secrets" then make sure your Inner Plan is VERY healthy.

An example may be the best way to understand the Inner Plan. Consider Mahatma Gandhi who, in the first half of the 20th century, had an Outer Plan to free India from colonial England. There was nothing secret about his goal, and he became a thorn in the side of England until eventually they relented and handed rule of India back to the Indian government in 1947. His Outer Plan fulfilled, what can we deduce about his Inner Plan?

His Inner Plan did not make the news as much as his Outer Plan, but to those who knew him and followed the events of his life his Inner Plan was about how well he could live by his own spiritual ideals. In other words, his Inner Plan was the plan of how he wanted to live, and he gave as much thought to it as he did his Outer Plan.

To determine your Outer Plan and it's goal the questions you would ask would be as follows: "What do I want to have?" and "What do I want to do?"

To determine your Inner Plan, the question is simple "How do I want to live my life?" With this question you begin to unfold the deeper values and motivations that you want to live by. When you become focused on this "How?" question you begin to see that your life is more than just achieving goals. Life starts to become about the values you want to personify.

I highly recommend that before you attempt creating your cult you unravel your own personal riddle by delving deep into the question of "*How* do I want to live my life?"

How To Find Out What You Want

Grab a pen and a piece of paper and start writing your answers to these questions:

- "What do I want to have?"
- "What do I want to do?"
- "*How* do I want to live my life?"

The key this psychological archeology is to not stop writing. Even if you end up repeating what you've written just keep at it. The end result you are looking for is not words on paper but a feeling of motivation, so keep at it.

Through this process you will gain a clarity of vision. As you do this daily, you will find out which hopes and desire remains consistent and which are more fleeting. You will also discover the values that you personally wish to live by.

Patience

Patience will yield you much as a virtue for a cult leader. IF everything is urgent and by being impatient you might be more likely to push harder to achieve your goals. Yes, perhaps that is true, and you can find many people who felt an urgency in the building of a loyal following. The question is "Is that urgency and impatience worth it?"

Unless you thrive on the frenetic pace of constant urgency I would recommend you hold strong to the big picture you created with your Plan. If you understand your Plan you understand that everything will happen in its own time. All you have to do is work the Plan. Obstacles and challenges may delay the fulfillment of the Plan but the Plan is inevitable.

If you think there is something you need to do to hasten the process you should be warned. This can be a pitfall for some cult leaders. The delusional Charles Manson believed the only way to start the great apocalypse was to kill people. He could have waited and worked to connect more people with his reality but he was impatient.

Impatience is understandable but not at the cost of destroying your dream.

Rational Objectivity

Rational objectivity is the ability to calmly respond to situations without allowing emotions to distract you. Rational objectivity is more of an ideal than a reality for most of us. We naturally are subject to emotional reactions, and often when we look back on how our emotional response helped the situation we find that it didn't.

Building Your Cult

Rational objectivity helps us by giving us time to think through how one course of action can help and another can hurt. All you have to do is think of the times a family member or boss exploded into anger and ask yourself if they could have responded better to get the result they wanted. Usually the answer is yes. Of course you should put yourself through the same scrutiny. By calmly looking back on your actions and evaluating their effectiveness you can consider options of what to do better.

Rational objectivity will also strengthen your ability to choose what is most efficient instead of what simply feels good. Anger may feel good but you are more than likely to alienate your supporters by being angry at them. Is it really your most effective and efficient response?

Rational objectivity will protect you from other potentially dangerous responses. Love can blind you to possible manipulation. Fear can exaggerate potential threats. Understand, you cannot stop yourself from feeling these emotions but your rational objectivity will make you aware of their dangers and give you more freedom to consider your options.

You should also be willing and eager to put yourself into challenging situations that allow you to practice your rational objectivity. Do this and, over time, you will gain that calm Olympian perspective that can give you the time you need to think of the right response.

Strengthening Your Rational Objectivity

One of the best exercises to instill rational objectivity is to think of automatic emotional reactions that

E motional
R eaction
I mpedes
C ontrol

www.BuildingYourCult.com

Building Your Cult

hinder your progress as your most hated enemy.

Remember that any emotion can pull you away from your Plan. Anger can blind, fear can exaggerate danger, even love can make you vulnerable to manipulation. The goal is not to avoid these feelings but to recognize their power and do everything necessary to keep you on your Plan.

Ways To Control Emotions

Think to the most recent time you allowed your emotions to control you. Think what would have been a better, more rational, response. In your mind, go back to that moment and practice a calm and rational response. Do this regularly until you do it to your satisfaction in real life.

It is likely that has a human being you will never truly "master" your emotions but by doing this process you will always be growing closer and closer to your ideal.

Obsession

It is safe to say that obsession is not considered the most healthy of mental states, but you cannot look at the great accomplishments of history without seeing obsession as an important driver. Niccolo Tesla, Albert Einstein, Thomas Edison, Bill Gates, Alexander The Great are only a few of the better known names. Consider any great business and you will find some level of obsession within the people who built it.

Every good cult leader has some form of obsession. The obsession itself is neither good nor bad. It is how well you direct your obsession that matters.

To create the mindset of a great leader every part of your life must be integrated toward achieving the Plan you have written for yourself. Be aware that your obsession will both attract and alienate people. That is the benefit and cost of your ambition.

One way of safely creating your own obsession to achieve

Building Your Cult

your goal is to consider how our lives are divided into three aspects: Thinking, Feeling and Doing. Seldom are those three aspects working in balance. Our thinking mind will work to collect information believing that if we have all the information we need we will then act. Thus our Feeling and Doing aspects are weak.

Our Feeling aspect may motivate us into action, but when it wanes we stop because we are then waiting for the right "feeling" in order to act. Or, one can jump into action without giving enough thought to what should be done.

Ways For Balancing Thoughts, Feelings, And Actions

For any of your goals consider what it would be like if your Thinking, Feeling and Doing aspects were in balance. You can do this as a type of meditation in the form of the following questions:

"Have I given detailed thought to the step I will take?"
"Am I over thinking it?"
"What feeling can I generate right now to move me into action?"
"Is my thinking, feeling and doing aspects in balance enough to move me into intelligent action?"

If you are *sincerely* interested in creating an obsession to achieve I created an audio CD called "The PsychoPathology of Success" that will show you how to do the job. Be warned - obsession has lead as many to their downfall as to the heights of achievement. If you would like you can order the CD at www.DeltaSuccessProgram.com. The CD is the fourth in the Delta

Building Your Cult

Success Series.

There is also a section of this book call "Unleash The Addict" that can be used to create addiction within yourself and others. As you read through "Unleash the Addict" please consider using the techniques for the betterment of people and not just to control them.

Your Life as A Saga

Before providing your group with a story that binds the group together you must first look at your own life as a great epic saga, a heroic quest.

By so doing you begin to see yourself in the great Plan that you have created. You don't have to tell others, but it's important to recite it to yourself to get a clearer idea of where you and your future goals fit together.

Your life story will be flexible and ongoing. It will describe your victories, your challenges and your frustration. Because your life is ongoing your story will always be in the process of being written.

As your great saga transpires you may share parts of it with others while making sure that you color it as dramatically as you need to. Parts of the story can be shared with the members of your cult.

There are many such stories that exist within corporations. Like the CEO who fearing bankruptcy flew to Las Vegas and bet everything on the roll of a roulette wheel...and won.

A friend of mine was describing an exercise he did while attending religious seminary. He was asked to take an event of his life and write it so it compared to something from the bible. He chose a trip his family went on and compared it to the exodus of the jews from Egypt. Your epic saga should be as bold.

When you are asked if these stories are true your answer can simply be that they are "true enough."

Building Your Cult

This idea of creating a personal saga of your life is so important and potentially so transformational that it's worth going into more detail.

The details appear when we examine in the themes of what is referred to as "The Hero's Journey". These themes can be life filters through which we see our own live.

What follows are the themes of the Hero's Journey as described by the late Joseph Campbell. They are to give us perspectives of how we can view our lives. You will find these themes within the stories of many cultures and religions.

Please, as you consider these themes imagine where the stories of your life would fit. These are *your* stories.

The Invitation

1. The Call to Adventure
The call to adventure is the point in a person's life when they are first given notice that everything is going to change, whether they know it or not.

2. Refusal of the Call
Often when the call is given, the future hero refuses to heed it. This may be from a sense of duty or obligation, fear, insecurity, a sense of inadequacy, or any of a range of reasons that work to hold the person in his or her current circumstances.

3. Supernatural Aid
Once the hero has committed to the quest, consciously or unconsciously, his or her guide and magical helper appears, or becomes known.

4. The Crossing of the First Threshold
This is the point where the person actually crosses into the field of adventure, leaving the known limits of his or her world and

venturing into an unknown and dangerous realm where the rules and limits are not known.

5. The Belly of the Whale
The belly of the whale represents the final separation from the hero's known world and self. It is sometimes described as the person's lowest point, but it is actually the point when the person is between or transitioning between worlds and selves. The separation has been made, or is being made, or being fully recognized between the old world and old self and the potential for a new world/self. The experiences that will shape the new world and self will begin shortly, or may be beginning with this experience which is often symbolized by something dark, unknown and frightening. By entering this stage, the person shows their willingness to undergo a metamorphosis, to die to him or herself.

Initiation

1. The Road of Trials
The road of trials is a series of tests, tasks, or ordeals that the person must undergo to begin the transformation. Often the person fails one or more of these tests, which often occur in threes.

2. The Meeting with the Goddess
The meeting with the goddess represents the point in the adventure when the person experiences a love that has the power and significance of the all-powerful, all encompassing, unconditional love that a fortunate infant may experience with his or her mother. It is also known as the "hieros gamos", or sacred marriage, the union of opposites, and may take place entirely within the person. In other words, the person begins to see him or herself in a non-dualistic way. This is a very important step in the process and is often represented by the person finding the other person that he or she loves most completely. Although Campbell symbolizes this step as a meeting

Building Your Cult

with a goddess, unconditional love and /or self unification does not have to be represented by a woman.

3. Woman as the Temptress
At one level, this step is about those temptations that may lead the hero to abandon or stray from his or her quest, which as with the Meeting with the Goddess does not necessarily have to be represented by a woman. For Campbell, however, this step is about the revulsion that the usually male hero may feel about his own fleshy/earthy nature, and the subsequent attachment or projection of that revulsion to women. Woman is a metaphor for the physical or material temptations of life, since the hero-knight was often tempted by lust from his spiritual journey.

4. Atonement with the Father
In this step the person must confront and be initiated by whatever holds the ultimate power in his or her life. In many myths and stories this is the father, or a father figure who has life and death power. This is the center point of the journey. All the previous steps have been moving in to this place, all that follow will move out from it. Although this step is most frequently symbolized by an encounter with a male entity, it does not have to be a male; just someone or thing with incredible power. For the transformation to take place, the person as he or she has been must be "killed" so that the new self can come into being. Sometime this killing is literal, and the earthly journey for that character is either over or moves into a different realm.

5. Apotheosis
To apotheosize is to deify. When someone dies a physical death, or dies to the self to live in spirit, he or she moves beyond the pairs of opposites to a state of divine knowledge, love, compassion and bliss. This is a god-like state; the person is in heaven and beyond all strife. A more mundane way of looking at this step is that it is a period of

Building Your Cult

rest, peace and fulfillment before the hero begins the return.

6. The Ultimate Boon
The ultimate boon is the achievement of the goal of the quest. It is what the person went on the journey to get. All the previous steps serve to prepare and purify the person for this step, since in many myths the boon is something transcendent like the elixir of life itself, or a plant that supplies immortality, or the holy grail.

The Return

1. Refusal of the Return
So why, when all has been achieved, the ambrosia has been drunk, and we have conversed with the gods, why come back to normal life with all its cares and woes?

2. The Magic Flight
Sometimes the hero must escape with the boon, if it is something that the gods have been jealously guarding. It can be just as adventurous and dangerous returning from the journey as it was to go on it.

3. Rescue from Without
Just as the hero may need guides and assistants to set out on the quest, often times he or she must have powerful guides and rescuers to bring them back to everyday life, especially if the person has been wounded or weakened by the experience. Or perhaps the person doesn't realize that it is time to return, that they can return, or that others need their boon.

4. The Crossing of the Return Threshold
The trick in returning is to retain the wisdom gained on the quest, to integrate that wisdom into a human life, and then maybe figure out how to share the wisdom with the rest of the world. This is usually

extremely difficult.

5. Master of the Two Worlds
In myth, this step is usually represented by a transcendental hero like Jesus or Buddha. For a human hero, it may mean achieving a balance between the material and spiritual. The person has become comfortable and competent in both the inner and outer worlds.

6. Freedom to Live
Mastery leads to freedom from the fear of death, which in turn is the freedom to live. This is sometimes referred to as living in the moment, neither anticipating the future nor regretting the past.

Building Your Cult

The Cult Organization

Work on yourself is to never stop. If you think you've ever reached a point of perfection you are dead wrong. Self improvement and self awareness is an ongoing process that should never stop.

After beginning the work on yourself (which I cannot recommend highly enough) it is time to think about the cult organization you want to build.

It is safe to say that most of what you'll learn about building and managing your cult will be learned on the job. That said, there are certain things for which you can prepare. This section is designed to give you that head start.

Asking the right questions is more important than anything. Be prepared, because if you do go through this section in detail you may successfully conclude that your desire to start a cult was nothing more than a poorly thought our attempt to satisfy a juvenile need for power. If that's the case then it's best to put your cult building desires on the back burner for awhile.

On the other hand, you might conclude that a cult is exactly what you deeply desire and need and that it would fulfill all your dreams. If so, good luck, and I promise it will be a wild ride.

Cult Purpose

To get anything done in life you have to intend to do it. Life doesn't happen by happenstance. The same is true if you want to form a cult. You have to intend to do it. But if all you have is a vague desire to have a cult it's likely that anything you do will fizzle for lack of any clear direction.

You cult has to (make that ***must, gotta, absolutely has to***) have a greater purpose than fulfilling your own personal need for power.

Building Your Cult

To discover your cult's purpose you need to discover your own purpose and meld the two into one. If your cult has a spiritual focus ask yourself how it will help fulfill your own spiritual ideals. If your cult consists of a long list of loyal customers then you need to be very, very clear as to how you will keep these cult members loyal.

Begin with paper and pencil and writing all the sentences you can that begin with the words "The purpose of my cult/group is to..." and keep doing it until you find the sentence(s) that touch you personally and would help fulfill both your Inner and Outer Plan.

You will need to find a purpose for your group that is inspired and glorious because you will use that feeling and sense of destiny to create a cult mythos that will inspire others.

Cult Mythos

A mythos is a set of stories that together create an identity for a culture or group of people.

If you've ever sat long with a Greek family (or any family with a rich cultural tradition) you can get the feeling that there is a pride they have for being of that tradition. A rich cultural tradition will include stories of heroes on dangerous adventures as well as victories they celebrate as part of that national culture. This cultural tradition will also include songs and slogans that help define that identity.

It is that sense of pride and identity that you want to instill in each member of your group, so it is up to you to begin the mythos, tell the stories that make your goals seem divinely inspired. Consider your story, or any story about your group, to be a story of heroes on a quest, or even divine beings fighting evil. When you do that the members begin to see themselves within the stories. Thus you learn

Building Your Cult

to make your stories to include as many types of heroic characters as possible.

Once you have an idea of the power of your cult mythos you can begin to solidify it with songs, slogans and images. The secret to making powerful propaganda is to link people of a certain quality with an image, song or slogan. War propaganda will show a heroic image of allies as gallant, noble and brave and reveal their enemies as spurious, craven and vile. This will ring throughout their songs and slogans as well.

Perhaps the most successful use of the cult mythos was in Nazi Germany. Hitler was so aware of the power of the cult mythos that he created a government agency called The Ministry of Propaganda. Upon overtaking a government Hitler's forces would embark on a massive propaganda campaign to instill the values of the Nazi party.

People often wonder how a nation became so intoxicated with the Nazi mythos, but all you have to do is see the propaganda that was created and imagine the constant and daily media bombardment of posters, songs and slogans. Hitler's goal was to create a national movement that was a combination of politics and religion. You can now look at the military recruiting posters from every nation and see that they learned to duplicate what Nazi Germany first mastered.

There are plenty of other examples of the effective use of mythos' application to propaganda. Consider CityYear, an organization dedicated to asking young people to volunteer a year of public service in order to help change the world. Their slogan is "Give a year. Change the World." CityYear builds it's image about figures of John F. Kennedy and Martin Luther King. When among

Building Your Cult

the CityYear volunteers it is easy to notice their idealistic youthful energy. Often their group meetings are like motivational workshops with all the members cheering and applauding encouragement.

Japanese corporate culture has also built a propaganda machine into its structure. New employees are well indoctrinated into their company's culture by making the company a part of the family. Companies have group exercises and company sports teams that employees are encouraged to take part in. These are not considered extracurricular activities, but a part of the corporate family. In this environment a person may give an 80, 90 or even a 100 hour work week. This concept was borrowed and modified by the modern computer industry who learned to take young energetic college graduates with little prior work experience and turn the company into a familiar campus setting where they would eat, sleep and dream work.

Processes That Maintain The Cult Structure

Let's make a distinction between process and content. The content is what you say, or the message of your cult. The process is HOW the message is delivered. Typically content creates information that people can discuss and share, doctrine for example. Process creates the experience they have about that information or doctrine.

When building your cult it is a good idea to give a lot of consideration to process.

This next step may require a new way of thinking in order to understand. Typically if you wanted a group of people to join a movement you would set goal, publicize what you're doing and encourage people to join you. The question then becomes how do you maintain the cohesiveness of the group and loyalty of the members?

The answer is in the subtle processes that take place within the group. These are the processes between members, between

Building Your Cult

different parts of the group, and between group members and people outside the group.

Process is not about what is done...but HOW it is done, and this can have an invisible but powerful affect on the people involved.

As an example, in order to instill a sense of reverence in its followers an ashram may require that everyone removes their shoes upon entering a shrine and to speak in low tones. Over time this will have a much more powerful affect than simply telling people, "this is a holy place."

Likewise, all the people in a courtroom are told "All rise!" when the judge enters, and he sits in a position that is higher than anyone else. This is the process used to instill the judge's authority, and without anyone having to say it. Are you starting to see the value and power of process?

Another example came from a motivational workshop I once attended. During the training the leader made it explicitly clear that when an exercise was introduced everyone was to respond with cheers and applause. He went the process several times saying to the audience "Let's do an exercise!" making sure everyone's energy was at 100%. If during the training people didn't respond enthusiastically enough he would stop, retrain them to respond correctly and then say again "Let's do an exercise!". By the end of the training everyone was looking back at the exercises as the most valuable part of the training. From this you the lesson is to teach your followers/employees/subordinates how to respond *explicitly* in any given situation. It will make your business run more smoothly.

In order to create processes that reinforces your cult's values you first must determine exactly what those values are and ask what rules of behavior would best instill those values. A good example is the idea of wearing uniforms. In the early days of IBM every employee was required to wear a suit, tie and hat to instill that they were part of the IBM family.

Building Your Cult

Cult Values

The Cult Values are those concepts and ideas that the cult deems as most important. If your cult is a business then your cult's values could be hard work and dedication to a dream. A religious cult could hold the values of devotion, selflessness, and service to the needy.

The list of potential cult values is long and great thought should be given to choosing which values best represents the cult you wish to create. If at some future point you think your cult's values should be altered then there might be some friction among those who are already involved. First, give good thought to the processes, the cult's values, and plan ahead.

Here is a list of possible Cult Values:

- Simplicity
- Obedience to doctrine
- Obedience to the leader or guru
- Truth of the doctrine
- Hard work
- Service
- Devotion

A business may wish to instill some of these values:

- Ingenuity
- Independent thinking
- Never use debt to create profit
- Manageable growth
- Elitism and Exclusive products

These lists can go on and on.

www.BuildingYourCult.com

Building Your Cult

Once you've determined your cult's values there are two ways to build your values into your cult. The first is to explicitly say, "this is what we value" and begin to teach around those explicit declarations.

The second is to make these values a part of the cult structure. This is the more subtle and more powerful method because it helps create experiences whose meaning represents those values.

For example if a slaughterhouse wants to instill the value of cleanliness among it's workers it would give people awards and bonuses based on the cleanliness of their work area.

Other companies who want their employees to be free-thinking problem solvers would simply give them a task to solve with minimal restrictions and set them to it. They will follow this up with regular problem solver awards.

Cult Doctrine

Regardless of the type of cult you create, cult doctrine will be an essential aspect to making the cult cohesive.

For a business, the cult doctrine would be it's operations manual and with it's statement of values included. An operations manual describes every practical aspect of how the business operates. When perfected the operations manual can be handed to a minimally trained employee and they can use it to do their job. Turn-key businesses like McDonald's and Kinko's sell their franchises based on the detail of their operations manual, so that anyone who can afford a franchise can start making money the minute they first open the door. That is the definition of a "turn key business" and should be the ideal of any organization you create.

For a religious group or spiritual movement the doctrine includes the texts that are used for worship or practice. These texts could also include the business aspects of the cult.

Building Your Cult

Most people understand cult doctrine as religious documents but that is only partly true. Bibles and documents contain the stories and myths of the cult, which is vital, but cult doctrine can also include the following cult aspects:

- Cult recruiting. On whom to focus recruiting efforts.
- The indoctrination process
- Cult hierarchy
- Codes of conduct
- Information control
- Public relations
- Cult income and business practices
- Business practices: where does the money go?
- Interacting with others inside and outside the group
- Rewards and Punishments

When cult doctrine is well thought out every point can be used to support every other point. This certainly can include the stories that make up the cult mythos.

One does not have to reinvent the wheel when it comes to most of cult doctrine. Many cults have been created whose single doctrine is the Old and New Testament. Variation of these doctrines have been spun off to fulfill the values of a multitude of cults. For business organizations their doctrine could be a formulaic business plan and operations manual.

This is where the Jews who follow the Talmud and Scientologists have a great deal in common: they both have detailed instructions by which their followers are to live. The Jews must separate their meat and dairy products and the Scientologists have to maintain regular auditing sessions to remain "clear". In all other ways they are quite different.

To understand this consider how that church tithing is supported by many scriptural references. Tithing becomes a part of

Building Your Cult

the mythos and business aspect of the religion. The exact same support can be created for any organization.

There are reported documents (doctrine) in Scientology that describes how to treat potential recruits in such a way that they are never given the chance to say "no," or to critically think about an offer. It describes how important it is to make this behavior a part of the Scientology culture. In this case the doctrine describes the desired behavior explicitly to support the cult's objectives.

Cult Structure and Cult Culture

Once you have established your cult's values and begun the creation of cult doctrine it is time to think of your cult as a structure that enforces those values.

Just like a business or a church it is very likely that your cult will have a hierarchy. A business has levels of management from the mail boy, administrative assistance, middle management, vice presidents all the way to the CEO. A church has clergy, laymen, and church members. There are plenty of people who will talk down the implementation of hierarchy in your organization, but as your cult grows it will be hard to do anything without some command structure. The point is to THINK IT THROUGH so that the cult will do what you want it to with a minimum of effort.

To get the best results you must instill your cult's values at every level of the cult hierarchy.

The Line Of Command

The line of command can be considered the path information travels back and forth between the leadership and the people in the field. It can also be used to describe the flow of resources and money.

Your line of command has two functions. The first is to simplify your work by creating a structure for delegating activities.

Building Your Cult

It's second function is to provide an efficient exchange of information up and down the command line. In this way you can have two or three people reporting to you instead of thirty and thus stave off any sense of overwhelm.

When creating your line of command and picking the people who will report to you it's important not to be seduced by one's resume. People are political animals and might well exploit their proximity to authority by secretly shunting money and resources their way. To help prevent this from happening be patient when selecting your subordinates and test them for ulterior motives and ambitions.

Ultimately your goal is to create clones of yourself as subordinates. These "clones" understand your thought process and decision strategies well enough to do things without being told. This way you can give your orders and let them accomplish the objective as they see fit. This takes a great deal of training so be patient and try to place these "clones" in key positions.

Some of the tests you can give these potential "clones" will be first to test their ambition by holding them back from projects they are eager to do. If they prove to be patient and subordinate to your orders you can begin to give them more power.

Another test is to give them an objective without instruction and see how they go about finishing the task. If they keep returning with the need for more instruction instead of thinking for themselves they're not ready. If the assignment gets bogged down in political infighting then they are not ready to be given a full leadership position.

Also it's important that they know they will always be tested. Being tested will either cause them to feel stress or motivate them to achieve. Take those who do well and enjoy this kind of pressure and assign them more projects to fulfill. They will naturally seek their own level of achievement and those who enjoy both the pressure to achieve and the freedom to accomplish these goals will become highly valued.

www.BuildingYourCult.com

Building Your Cult

For those people who respond to being tested with stress you'll find they're best suited for simple and repetitive jobs in your cult. Giving them a "simple" job should in no way be considered a demotion. Instead you and your cult needs to paint every position within it as vital to the success of the group. When people within these repetitive jobs want to change their position or responsibilities let them know that they must be tested, and see if they are up to the task.

Just as a business will grow to create corporate divisions such as marketing, payroll, human resources, research and development, etc., it's important to understand how your cult will grow so that you can create the necessary divisions. In each division a skilled person, a "clone" of yourself, is to be in place in order to accomplish the cult's objectives.

Cult Values And The Line of Command

The cult's values need to be enforced at every point within the line of command. So, if your organization values thrift and economy then every person within in it needs to demonstrate how they are saving the group money and furthering efficiency. It is not enough to point out who is doing badly, or wasting money, for this only creates animosity within the group and encourages a culture of whistle blowing. You must reward and encourage positive demonstrations of the cult values.

Consider the values you want to instill in your cult and how they will be acknowledged when people within the cult demonstrate them.

Creating a Group Bond

Getting your cult to act cohesively

Relationship expert John Gottman has determined that there are some very simple things couples can do to stay bonded, and they apply very well to larger groups. Here they are as adapted for larger

Building Your Cult

groups:

- Parting and End Of Day Stress Reduction

Parting simply means saying "goodbye" in a kind and respectful way. The End Of Day Stress Reduction could simply be a 20 minute group meeting where people can shake off the stresses of the day, give and receive acknowledgment for their efforts, and tell them that they are appreciated as people and as vital parts of a great plan.

In this End Of Day Stress Reduction only smiles, appreciation and applause are allowed.

- Group Outings

The group outing is the group equivalent of a weekly date. It involves all the cult members being part of an event that is unrelated to their other duties and is designed to be fun. When doing larger group outings it will be natural for cliques to form so it's the job of the outing organizers to intermix the people and prevent isolation from occurring between members and groups of members.

These things can be explicit and even be stated in various cult doctrine such as "Codes of Conduct" and "Group Outings." By stating up front that group outings are mandatory and that everyone is held to a code of conduct you leave out any

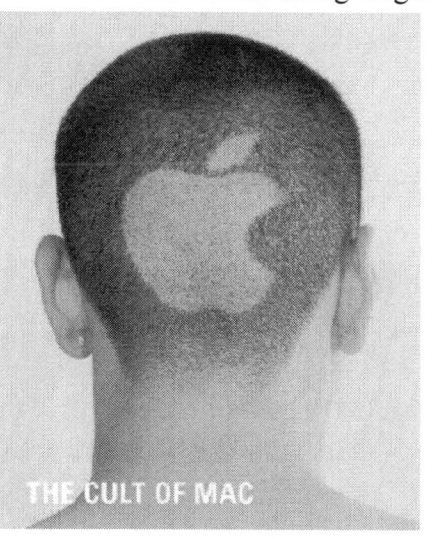

Building Your Cult

ambiguity of what is expected. Doing this will make it so that grumblers will be quickly noticed and dealt with accordingly.

Elitism

Elitism is the sense that in some way you, your cult and it's members are better than the uninitiated. It's a natural feeling that helps people feel special and unique. One of the benefits of elitism in a cult is in how it unifies it's members.

Apple computers make no apology for believing that it makes the best computers in the world. Whether they do or not isn't important, but every apple user feels they are part of a special class of computer user. The same is true of people who own and ride Harley-Davidson motorcycles. That is the feeling you want your followers to have.

Several steps can be taken to instill a sense of elitism. Each of these will be described in detail.

- Have a special mission, purpose or destiny
- Make it difficult to join
- Create initiations
- Have secret knowledge that is only for insiders.
- Create mysterious and unprovable rumors
- Incorporate membership into each individual's personal saga

Special Mission, Purpose or Destiny

Each cult should have some sort of special mission. The first part of a cult's mission can be stated as "save the world by..." or "make the world's best..." or "spread the gospel of..." The second part of a mission statement is to describe *how* you will fulfill your mission. You remove many ambiguities by describing how the mission statement will be fulfilled.

For example, the criminal gang cult Aryan Brotherhood

Building Your Cult

created the mission statement of becoming a major criminal organization through illegal drugs sales and extortion, and to do it by means of violence and coercion.

The mission statement of an internet entrepreneur might be as follows "to generate $$$ income over time through sales of my books online and to increase my subscriber database at least 10,000 people every year."

Make It Difficult To Join

Nothing makes something more appealing than telling someone they can't have it. This is the rule of scarcity. Likewise, when you discourage someone from joining your cult it makes it more interesting to them. Here are some ways to do that.

- Tell people it is best to not join the cult, and without telling them why.

- Tell them that it is definitely not for everyone, and they should think about it. Tell them to ask again at a later time.

- Tell them they would make a good candidate to join the cult, but you don't know if they would be able to withstand the initiation period.

- Tell stories of good candidates who failed the initiation period.

- Tell them that they are going to be asked to join the cult, only later tell them that you spoke too quickly and that it's not likely to happen.

Building Your Cult

Create Initiations

The reason cults (and many other groups) have initiation ceremonies is to help people have an experience that is exclusive to members of the group, and thereby create a sense of community. The initiation can take many forms.

1. The Quest. The initiate must travel on a journey to acquire or achieve something.
2. The Sentinel. The initiate must guard a location.
3. Trial by Interrogation. The initiate is questioned for the right answer.
4. Trial by Pain. Common in gangs, the initiate is beaten for 60 seconds by members.
5. Initiation by Assignment. The initiate is given an objective to accomplish. His membership depends on the outcome.

Secret Knowledge Only Insiders Know

Secret knowledge, or information given exclusively to members, gives people a feeling of being special and part of an elite group. The forms that secret knowledge often take include...

- The details of certain initiations. You can give the initiation rituals mysterious names which can be shared, but the details are to be secret.
- Having members create a cult name that is only to be shared with other members.
- Secret signs and handshakes.

Create Mysterious And Unprovable Rumors

Rumors have proven to be much more powerful than facts because they create curiosity and sometimes envy and fear to those

Building Your Cult

who hear them. That your group is subject to rumors – which no one will confirm or deny – makes those holding the secrets feel special.

Managing a rumor is a combination of creating the right rumor and telling people how to respond when asked about these rumors. Creating the rumor is the difficult part because it can easily get out of hand.

One of the better ways to create a rumor is to tell a story about something that *you* heard from someone else. This makes it hearsay but it is the frequency (not the veracity) of a rumor that gives it power. Because it's a story, you cannot confirm or deny it, and neither can those to whom it is told. The key is to make the rumor both amazing and plausible. A good rumor might describe how a member of the cult did something amazing, miraculous and beyond the norm because of the cult's teaching.

Membership And The Individual's Personal Saga

It is said that cults can be divided into two types: cults of confession and cult of testimonial.

Cults of confession rely on fear, shame and guilt to enforce members' compliance. Cults of testimonial rely on people telling their personal story of how the cult has help them.

Cults of confession are easy to create by simply exploiting people's need for approval and fear of rejection. The typical cult of confession has regular public confessions, not unlike an Alcoholics Anonymous meeting. The long term results, however, leave a lot to be desired. Every cult of confession has a vast colony of disgruntled ex-cult members who resent having being coerced into spying on their peers and confessing to their own "sins."

A more positive alternative is the cult of testimonial where members publicly talk about what they have learned and the benefits they've gained from the cult. These testimonials can include personal accomplishments, helpful things members have done for others, and the gratitude for having the cult in their life.

Building Your Cult

The end result of being in a cult of testimonial is that these stories become a part of person's personal saga, and so that when they reflect on them privately they feel good. This is very common among Christian youth cults where young people take turns telling the group how their lives have changed since knowing Jesus. This behavior can also be seen during public business promotions where the recently promoted employee describes how their dream has grown into a reality as they have worked at the company.

A very overt exercise to help merge cult membership into the person's story is to ask cult members to write "the story of their lives" as though it were an epic saga, but with attention to how their life changes as a result of having joined the group. This gives them the chance to see themselves as their own version of Luke Skywalker who are destined to concur an empire.

Commitment And Consistency

In his book Influence Robert Cialdini described how when people agree to do small things they are more likely to agree to bigger requests later on. This is known as the the rule of "commitment and consistency."

Commitment and consequences can be easily exploited in a cult by asking the membership for small donations of their time before ever asking them to give money.

Corporations employ this tactic by gradually asking more and more of salaried employees until they find themselves working an 80 hour week and believing it is what they had originally agreed to.

Scientology has mastered this process in what they call "The Training Routines" or TRs. The TRs are considered the start of any Scientology communication training

Building Your Cult

and are presented in a "gradient," with each step being an additional learning and also requiring more of the student. At the end of the Training Routines the student will be practicing giving commands to fellow students until they follow each command. This is referred to as a "Tone 40" command. Each student is also required to learn how to respond to a Tone 40 command without questioning it. Ultimately, when the communication training ends each student will be told (not asked) to sign up for further training. Because each student has been thoroughly trained to follow commands through "commitment and consistency" they gladly hand over huge sums of money to do the followup training.

The process is simple to implement. First have an ideal behavior which will be the most that you would want someone to do. Then create a small and simple behavior that most people would agree to do. After the cult member has agreed to do the first step make small incremental requests that ask for more each time. Each time the request is fulfilled thank them and show your appreciation, but the rewards need not be escalated in the same way as the requests. Soon the member will be willing to do the ideal desired behavior.

Human Resources And Man Management

You have to give those people in human resources a huge amount of praise and compassion. These are the people that deal with your most valuable and volatile commodity...people.

To be clear, Human Resources has the unenviable task of recruiting, placing and training people within your cult. It doesn't matter if it's a business or a church group – if your cult is small it will be you who must take on this task, and many others, until you have trained the right people to do the work for you.

While every cult has it's own hierarchy you can consider the responsibilities of your HR division to be as follows:

Building Your Cult

- Recruiting
- Indoctrination
- Reinforcement
- Removal

Recruiting

Getting people into your cult is the business of recruiting, and this should be thought of **as a business**. It's not about making friends but about getting the right people in the right position.

For a religious cult it starts with creating a flock and then a business to support it. The flock can be quite large before needing to create various positions to assist in its cult operations.

If your cult is a business with the hopes to generate a profit, then usually one should start with a small number of members or employees and grow only as fast as profits can sustain it.

There are many ways to recruit, and not all of them are suitable for every type of cult. A business may recruit by traditional business means like help wanted signs, want ads and recruiting services. A religious cult may recruit by having it's members do public service work, handing out pamphlets or inviting friends to attend services.

Let's make it clear if you are cult leader you need followers. The type of follower you need is entirely dependent on the type of cult you want. If your cult is a business you want loyal buyers. If your cult is a spiritual or self improvement movement you want like minded people. If your cult is based around your skills as an entertainer then you want loyal fans.

Cult leaders in addition to their desire for power are typically lazy and don't want to work at things that don't fulfill their destiny (this is a general description and not a judgment). Knowing this, you can begin to find your followers anywhere you would normally go. Your interests are their interests and vice versa. There is no reason

Building Your Cult

to waste your time looking for followers in places where you wouldn't want to go. So don't go to a monster truck rally looking for recruits to your self improvement cult. The only exceptions to that are 1) you like monster truck rallies or 2) your self improvement cult has something to do with monster trucks.

So consider your options. First, what do you like to do that is related to your cult? Do you have a strong spiritual belief or a rigorous meditative practice? Then it's very likely you will be attending related events which are perfect places to find potential followers. All you need to do is offer further trainings or group study events. The result will be you indulge your personal interest and begin your cult following.

If want to build a business cult, your first order of business is to know your business. If this means attending vocational school or taking classes you will be surrounded with fellow students likely interested in a business like yours.

My first visit to one dentist was a good example of a business cult. The service was friendly and lacking for nothing and when each of the employees began to talk about their employment they described it as being part of their "family". The dentist welcomed me with a hearty "Thanks for joining us" and went into how they are now happy to be responsible for all my dental care. Even when I left the receptionist took the time to say "We're glad to have you as a part of our family."

While this treatment may seem a bit creepy to a some people, to the people who respond to it is like they have found a new home. A home filled with all the people needed to keep them smiling... literally. There are plenty of people willing to fork over money for that kind of treatment.

Indoctrination

Indoctrination is the process that converts an outsider to a full fledged member of the cult, and converts them in such a way that

Building Your Cult

they **feel** like a member and no longer like an outsider. This includes knowing some of the cult's inner secrets and responding in the proper cult way to various situations.

The most important part of the indoctrination process is getting the new cult member to connect with the cult's greater purpose or destiny. When this happens the member sees his or her destiny and the cult's destiny as one and the same. This is what motivated so many people during the growth of Silicon Valley. They could see that they were part of something progressive that would help create a new type of world.

Consider indoctrination to be like the six month probation period of a new job or what happens when one joins a college fraternity that combines hazing and education.

To create your indoctrination process consider what you want your new cult member to think, feel and believe about the cult, and begin designing trainings they'll have, documents (doctrine) to read, and experiences they can go through.

Every new recruit, just like a new employee, has to be trained, so let your training include both information and exercises that enforce cult beliefs, doctrine and goals. It is important to note that many successful invisible cults put more energy into teaching beliefs, doctrine and goals than teaching job duties.

The beginning of the indoctrination process must instill two feelings within the initiate: the feeling of being accepted and the feeling of being challenged. Being accepted makes them want to stay within the cult. Being challenged motivates them to do more for the cult.

Acceptance

The typical method for creating a sense of acceptance is referred to as "love bombing." This is a process in which the new initiate is given hugs, smiles, kind words and praise for joining and for "towing the line."

Building Your Cult

In a business a new employee should be given everything mentioned above that is short of violating sexual harassment laws. New employees begin to look forward to each day at work. New cult members begin to feel the cult is more of a family to them than their own biological family.

To institute "love bombing" it should be incorporating into the doctrine and mythology. In this way it soon becomes a part of the cult's culture.

Challenge

A sense of challenge can be utilized by giving the initiate lots of detailed but important instructions. This will test their limits and motivate them in a positive way to work hard.

When challenging people it's a good idea to recognize that different people have different limits. Some like to be pushed hard, while others need a more gentle nudging.

When acceptance and challenge are combined they can create a very motivated and hard working cult member, and that's the desired result of an effective HR department.

The Non-Disclosure Agreement (NDA)

Depending on your cult it might be worth requiring a non-disclosure agreement (NDA) for some, maybe all, aspects of the cult.

A non-disclosure agreement will add a sense of importance to what they are doing and make them part of the "inner circle" of people "in the know." This would have the affect of reinforcing the elitism of the cult.

For the cult an NDA has the force of a legal agreement to keep cult secrets safe. It is also something that can be dangled over the head of possible whistle blowers.

Reinforcement

Reinforcement is also an important job for your cult's HR team because it keeps existing cult members happy and excited about continuing their service. Reinforcement consists of three parts:

- Reminding each member of their importance to the cult
- Asking for sacrifice
- Rewarding and keeping members' bellies full.

Reminding Each Member Of Their Importance

Having a destiny for you cult is critically important. With a destiny you can show people their place is the Great Plan, and allow them to feel as if they are more than just a cog in a big machine.

This can be done in a step by step fashion by first reiterating the cult's mission and then by describing **in detail** how their job is vital to the cult's mission. The detail they are offered must show the consequences their actions have to the Great Plan. In other words, they must see, hear and feel their own importance to the mission.

Ask For Sacrifice

The sacrifice could be big or small. It may mean simply asking them to do a simple task, or it could be asking them to perform to a much higher standard. Either way it must be presented as significant and instrumental to the cult's mission.

The combination of reinforcing their importance and asking

Building Your Cult

for sacrifice might sound something like the following:

"We have a great mission and I want you to be part of it. We want to (mission statement) and your job of licking envelopes is important. These letters are going out to everyone in our membership so that they can all (something) and without your effort none to this is going to happen."

"That is why I've got to ask you, in order for us to make our mission a reality, are you willing to seal all of these letters by the end of the day?"

Reward Them And Keep Their Bellies Full

This concept is sadly overlooked by many religious and spiritual cults. They believe that because they are providing a non-material service they should give only non-material rewards. There are plenty of reports of cult members being starved and denied any benefit for their effort then being chastised for not be grateful enough..

One spiritual cult that is famed for supporting it's members is the Mormon Church (also known as The Church of Latter Day Saints or LDS Church). The LDS Church has all sorts of offshoot businesses and services that are tailored for those who respond affirmatively when asked, "are you a member of the church?" During hardship a loyal Mormon can be assured they won't go unfed and forgotten.

For a business cult the typical reward is simply a paycheck, and this falls under the category of "keeping their bellies full." However, it is by not the only means of reward. In addition to a respectable paycheck always try to determine other ways you can augment their good work. This could be praise, a title change, promotion, group acknowledgment or a gift bonus.

Removal

Removing a cult member from the group is the most unenviable task for anyone who has worked in human resources. Until you have someone you can delegate to this distasteful job it will be in your hands.

Many cults remove people with little concern about the repercussions and follow it up by shunning the the person they dismiss. On the one hand it's understandable why some cults might act so strict with non-believers. On the other hand it can make for some really bad public relations (then again, some say any publicity is good publicity).

Removal from the cult is best when it's not arbitrary and emotional. Sure, it may appease the whims of the cult leader (you) but the long term results probably won't help.

The ideal method of removal can come in several forms.

The member could be asked to leave, When asking the member to leave the cult it should be done in a very warm and compassionate fashion, and by pointing out that the fit is not perfect and that the member might do much better in a different setting. Then present to them the specifics that show why it's a poor fit. Wish them well and give them **some** support if they agree to leave.

If asking them to leave the cult doesn't get the desired result then the process can be escalated. Continue to maintain a compassionate tone, only this time after explaining what they are doing wrong tell them that their work is no longer needed. You will help them with the transition and give them the deadline when they must leave.

Don't be surprised if they react emotionally. Remain calm

because it's always best to get them out without having to escalate the situation.

Lastly, people will come and go from your cult all on their own. There is little reason to compel them to stay if they don't want to be there. If you use guilt, anger or coercion to keep them it will eventually come back to haunt you and your reputation. If someone wants to leave, find out what you can learn from them so it's less likely to happen to others in the future. Then let them go.

Advanced HR Training

It may become necessary to train the Human Resource personnel to do advanced training of cult members. This could be used to engage members in such a way that they feel compelled to serve or become addicted to the cult. The appendix includes a section called "Unleash The Addict" that has very advanced NLP processes that can be used to create powerful feelings of want and desire in cult members.

Before jumping to the appendix I encourage you to be cautious with what you learn from this book. Being too eager to apply what you learn may release more monsters than you're capable of controlling.

The Motivational Imperative

The Motivational Imperative is the concept of creating a single goal that motivates every action of life. This goal acts as a "have to" whenever anyone makes a choice or decision. The idea originated from a science fiction TV show in which extraterrestrial aliens programmed their human servants to protect their "masters" at all costs. This Motivational Imperative to serve and protect would override even ones choices for self preservation.

Let us understand that a Motivational Imperative is only a concept and while it can be a romantic ideal of leaders and managers

Building Your Cult

it does not exist in reality. But, as a concept it is useful.

The Motivational Imperative has it's benefits and hazards.

The greatest benefit comes when the cult leader creates a motivational imperative within themselves, especially if the imperative is supportive of their health, life and well being. As an example *"I will always remember that I am loved and act toward my life purpose."* can be a very healthy Motivational Imperative.

The hazards of a Motivational Imperative come when the cult leader becomes too specific with his Imperative as this can create obsessive behaviors that limit choices.

Having too many parts of a Motivational Imperative can create confusion. Just like everyone likes to believe that laws are simple and clear cut there reality reveals a mass of complexities.

Motivational Imperatives have even more hazards when you attempt to create them in your followers.

Firstly, people are not machines nor are they programmable like computers. Intentionally creating a Motivational Imperative in someone is a hit or miss endeavor. The most consistent Motivational Imperative that cults have created relies heavily on fear, guilt and shame. It is a risky endeavor with more potential hazards than benefits... oh, and it's highly unethical too but keep in mind that many religions have their own form of Imperatives in the form of *"Thou shalt..."*.

Another obstacle in creating a Motivational Imperative in someone else is that it's hard to enforce it so that it permeates every part of your followers life. If your follower has a tendency toward obsessive-compulsion then perhaps it's possible but do your ***really*** want someone with a mental disorder following your every word?

Now the question comes can you create a Motivational Imperative in someone using hypnosis and focus on positive feelings? The answer is yes but you will still have to deal with the possible ethical dilemma it creates. I would encourage any leader to always focus on creating positive feelings and focusing them toward constructive actions.

Building Your Cult

Doctrine

Doctrine provides several essential functions. It encourages and discourage certain behaviors and creates useful rules for interacting with the world. The Doctrine of this book is designed to help you empower yourself to create a loyal following of supporters, if that is your desire. If it is not your wish to start a cult the Doctrine will still be of use in some way.

When creating a doctrine it needs to have two qualities. The first quality is that it has to be simple enough that people can remember it and easily find applications in their daily lives.

The second quality of doctrine is that it needs to be deep enough that it can be explored, expounded upon and debated. This will appeal to the intellectual aspect of the mind. By debating and expounding upon these "simple truths" people give their own meaning to doctrine and provide fertile ground for those in the future who will be pondering them. To understand the importance of depth, consider how much has been written and debated about the ten commandments, or the 12 steps of AA. Also consider how Buddhist doctrine starts with The Four Noble Truths and The Eight Fold Path but now there are over 2000 years of discourse and variation on those themes of Buddhism.

Once the doctrine is established it needs to become "solid." The way to do this is to provide rituals, songs, stories and slogans that incorporate the doctrine. Doing this provides simple ways people can incorporate doctrine into their lives.

What follows is the Doctrine of this book. I ask that you consider each step and apply it as you see fit. Feel free to modify it to better suit you.

Building Your Cult

The Doctrine Of This Book

Remembering that doctrine must first be simple yet have enough content to offer opportunities for discussion and elaboration.

The simplicity of this books doctrine can be remembered by simply counting One, Two, Three and Many:

- One Person
- Two Promises to Remember
- The Three Internal Forces
- The Many parts of the person

The doctrine continues to deal with "The World."

- Your Destiny
- Create A Mythos
- The World
- Propaganda
- Your Cult
- The Trinity of Suffering

The One Person

The individual is the One Person. All things happen to One Person...YOU. *"No matter where you go you have to take yourself, and you will always be there when you arrive."* Thus you, the individual, the One Person, must give yourself love and support no matter what.

The One Person is made greater by a personal sense of purpose and destiny. Do not wait around for some purpose to befall you. Now... right now ... is the time that you can choose your purpose and your destiny. When you do that your life will change from that point on.

Building Your Cult

Destiny is the unique and certain belief that you are the single person around which something wonderful will transpire. Destiny is more than a goal or a want. It is the ultimate outcome of your life. Make every effort to envision your destiny in as much detail as possible, making it compelling and important.

It is you, the One Person, who can choose and build your destiny.

From the time of his birth he felt both a part of something and different from everything. Nowhere could he explain adequately.

With his family he grew to feel connected to them but in some way different. When they laughed and smiled, he laughed and smiled. During the time the family was in stress and sorrow he felt that as well but he also felt that he was not meant for that.

He knew he could go further and do more.

He knew that there was a way so that the ordinary and worldly experiences could be transcended and improved.

Where ever he went he knew this to be true and even as he slept the thoughts would invade his dreams and remind him that he alone could solve his problems.

Then one day he made that promise to accept the responsibility for his life.

The Two Promises To Remember

There are Two Promises that can build and guide the One Person to their destiny.

- The Promise to remember that you are loved.
- The Promise to remember that you have a greater destiny.

The Promise To Remember That You Are Loved

As humans we often have a personal history of sabotaging

Building Your Cult

ourselves. We want love but we fear possible rejection. We seek power but we don't take risks. We feel guilt or shame just for having desires, and the end result is that we hold back.

To be loved is to be accepted...completely accepted. The first love the One Person (you) must have is the love and acceptance for yourself. Love and acceptance of yourself is not vainglory or pride. It is a practical way to bring together all the divergent and sabotaging aspects of the personality and direct them all towards your destiny.

The parts of us that are inner saboteurs may work against us, but beneath the surface they hold a positive intent. We may all want to be thin but the positive intent of over eating is indulgence in the pleasure we get from food. Even the practice of self-mutilation ("cutting") is used to distract one's self from anxiety. While these parts may overtly hurt they do in fact have our happiness in mind. They are just going about it in a destructive way. By loving these parts of ourselves they are more likely to hear our pleas.

Our pleas to these multitudes of inner saboteurs might sound much like this:

"I love you completely and ask you to hear me. I know your desire is to help, support and please me in your own way and now I'm asking you to change. I love you and am asking you to work for me in a new way so that you and I may accomplish our great destiny together."

Saying words like these to yourself repeatedly with loving emotion will eventually soften the offending parts. Eventually that "part" is no longer separated from "you." Instead, it is welcomed back like the prodigal son. In so doing you become a whole and unified person with **every** part of you now working toward your destiny.

If your inclination is to theistic belief then you can substitute you loving yourself for your deity loving you. One cult leader told

Building Your Cult

me in private, *"I'm sure God loves me. As much as I've prayed for it all my evidence has shown me that I can demonstrate that love a little better than God."*

As he slept one night he saw in the distance an object that that stood as tall as his head. As he approached he saw the picture of a man on the object and felt a kindness and peacefulness to the image.

Approaching closer he could see the details of the mans appearance and his heart grew warmer at the image. The image reassured him and he notice the smile on the mans face and the welcoming look and as he smiled more so did the image of the man until he broke out into laughter for he realized object was a long mirror and the man was his reflection.

At that moment the mirror disappeared but the man remained and the two walked close to laugh and embrace.

The dream ended with him laughing with tears in his eyes. Never had he felt so loved and accepted.

The Promise To Remember Your Greater Destiny

Know first that you have a destiny, and then make perfectly clear in your mind what that destiny is.

Your destiny is the polar star that guides you. Every action, every thought and choice will either bring you closer to your destiny or get you nowhere.

Take extreme care with who you decide to share your destiny, or better yet, share it with no one. You will then prevent anyone from sabotaging your destiny or misunderstanding you.

The more clearly you can envision your destiny the more swiftly you will achieve it. The clarity of your destiny includes the details of what you will accomplish, how you will do it and when it will be accomplished. It also includes the type of person you will become as you accomplish it.

Building Your Cult

By returning again and again to the vision of your destiny you can begin to program your mind. In a process unique to the human mind you will begin to direct every action towards your goal by uniting the Three Internal Forces of man: Thinking, Feeling and Doing.

From an early age he knew that somehow he was different but he did not know how and this feeling carried with him until that time when he realized he had a choice. He could live his life like those around him, like his friends and family, and fit into a predictable routine where all he had to do is what he knew others did or he could choose his own path.

He then chose. Even though at that moment he did not know the direction of his life he knew it would one different from anyone else. He also knew that until he discovered his purpose in life he would act and behave as though he knew it all along.

From that point on his life was never the same.

The Three Internal Forces

There are three internal force within your control that will propel you toward your destiny and help you keep the Two Promises – your thoughts, your emotions, and your actions.

To be most effective these forces must be in balance with each force having it's use and application. If a human uses one of these forces at the exclusion of any other then nothing will be accomplished.

Thus, to achieve a great destiny your thoughts, emotions and actions need to be united toward that goal.

With a sense of destiny you will be able to examine every thought, feeling and action and evaluate how useful it will be to you. If it will help you then you use it. If is but a trifling distraction you can choose to let it go.

www.BuildingYourCult.com

Building Your Cult

Upon accepting the challenge to rule his life he began examine his life more critically. His thoughts, feelings and actions each would pull him in one direction or another. Sometimes he felt lazy and unmotivated, other times insecure and hesitant and still other times he recognized he was moody and sullen.

He would find times of fluid creativity and momentum only to have it halted by anger or obsession.

As a man of purpose and destiny he knew that to control his life he must master himself.

Thinking

Thinking is the intellectual aspect of achievement. To accomplish great things intentionally you must think through how you will achieve it. The more thought you give to planning your destiny the more you will understand the details of every step and the easier your efforts will be.

But thinking by itself will not move you into action with desire, and a thought will not lift a spoon or shape a granite block. The other two forces must be activated.

To be romanced by thought alone will leave you a collector of information with not enough desire to act. People who lean too heavily on thought alone are always hoping to get more information, believing that at some point the information alone will compel them into action.

At times he was lost in thought and detail. The obsession would help him complete his planning but it would also prevent him from acting swiftly.

Feeling

Feeling is what puts us into motion. Emotions are the keys to motivation, and we are motivated by either pleasure or by pain, or a combination of the two. When you generate the right feeling at the right time **anyone** can be influenced to act...even in ways beyond their normal behavior. Why? Because is feels right.

There are people who are driven by their emotions. On a good day when they "feel" like it they can be very creative. Their creative feelings can be wonderful when they happen, but there can be long stretches where they won't act because they simply don't "feel like it." These people can be creative but fickle.

Controlling the force of feelings and emotions can be a challenge, but is well worth the effort. Negative emotions which do not help you can be spotted and halted. Positive emotions which move you into action can be nurtured.

He saw people who were so afflicted with emotion they could not act due to melancholy. They were dedicate to action only when it "felt" right. They were creative when healthy but lapsed into stagnation at the slightest decent of mood.

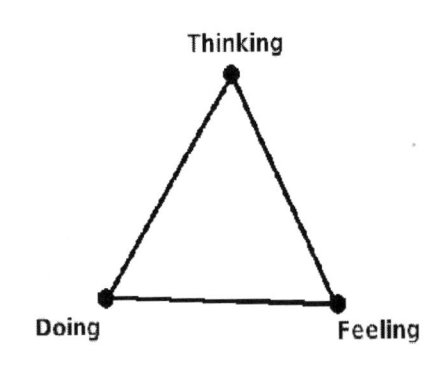

Doing

The last of the triad of forces is doing, or action. You can have thought out all the details, made all of the plans and worked yourself into a frenzy of excitement, but if you don't act then nothing will happen.

There are people who love being active. In fact, they will throw themselves into action without having thought things through. They love starting projects, but seldom maintain the momentum to complete them because they can't hold on to the joy.

When the three forces of thinking, feeling and doing are

united and balanced then everything falls into place. Nothing is wasted. Any action taken has the force of being well thought through and is backed by powerful emotions. Emotion is sustained over time by strength of will.

With these forces united there is no waste of thought, emotion and action, and things seem to move for you in greased grooves. Then there are no accidents, but everything that happens works towards your clearly defined destiny.

Awareness of Thoughts, Feelings and Actions

Set a goal that is important to you and ask yourself this question, *"In order to accomplish my goal what would be the best thoughts, feelings and actions so that I can complete it most efficiently."* Meditate on that question and go through every permutation of thought, feeling and action until you find the one that suits you best. Consider that the best result will allow you to maintain your focus and enthusiasm in the most effective way.

The three forces of thinking, feeling and doing, when sharpened to their heights, become the values and virtues of Wisdom, Love and Purpose.

Wisdom is the culmination of thoughts as they are applied to life. Love is the unconditional acceptance that comes from knowing yourself and appreciating every aspect of your life, past, present and future without exception. Purpose is a quality of action that extends itself far into the future. Together they create a person into a force of nature.

Everything became an opportunity to learn about the self. When he set a goal to accomplish he would measure the forces within him and determine what he needed to do and to learn to accomplish his goals most efficiently.

At other times speed was more important than efficiency and he would bring all his forces to bare to see how quickly his goal

Building Your Cult

would be achieved.
What he learned was the malleability of the human forces and how they can be manipulated to his aid.

The Many

The Many is the legion of desires, hopes, wants, weaknesses, fears and shames that drive and compel us away from our goals. It is the Many that distracts us from our destiny.

When the many are united together and focused toward a goal then there is no more distraction from reaching your destiny.

Many people look at The Many as an enemy. They feel guilt, anger and shame at these parts and treat them like demons to be exorcised. The result of this course of action is more guilt, anger and shame...not very helpful.

As mentioned in the Two Promises it is not guilt, nor anger that will exorcise these demons, because they are not demons at all. They are parts of us doing the very best they can to help us. Like well meaning children with poor training they don't know a better way to create happiness. The fastest and kindest way to change "The Many" is neither through anger nor guilt but through acceptance and love.

As young man he was moved by both desires and fears. Some were the passions of youth or the uncertainties of the future. One desire compelled him to act and another desire would distract him.

Setting any goal became an initiatory challenge. To stay focused meant to leash his desires.

Uniting The Many

The purpose of the following exercise is to bring together The Many for the end of helping you instead of hindering you. It is to be done as a private ritual with no one around because it is all

Building Your Cult

about you. The secret of being successful with this exercise or ritual is to take it very seriously and to do it as often as you need to.

The details of the ritual are up to you, but what you are to is perform a marriage ritual for yourself and on yourself that unites all of The Many parts together in love. Within the nurturing setting of this holy ceremony ask all The Many parts to make a vow to love and support you and your efforts. In return vow to The Many that you will in return continue to love them and nurture them in healthy and supportive ways.

When he saw how his many desires could distract him he redoubled his efforts and began to think of his life as a single great accomplishment that he is destined to fulfill.

Destiny

Destiny is more than a goal. Destiny is a purpose that drives your life. Destiny is the undying certainty that your are the central point around which great things will happen.

If you do not know your destiny or a destiny has not been given to you then your job is to find one.

If you have not found your destiny they you may start by simply assuming or knowing that you have one. Your destiny is waiting for you to be discovered. You MUST understand this with certainty, and your life will unfold like magic. That is where you can start. Anything can be chosen as your destiny so long as it is something that has meaning.

You must work to build **yourself** to to be the ideal person to fulfill your destiny.

With his destiny set chaos could not altered the outcome, only how it would come about.

Building Your Cult

The Trinity of Suffering

However, within the positive doctrine of health and happiness there rests the trinity of suffering. Take note of the following so as to not fall into a negative trap while constructing your cult's doctrine.

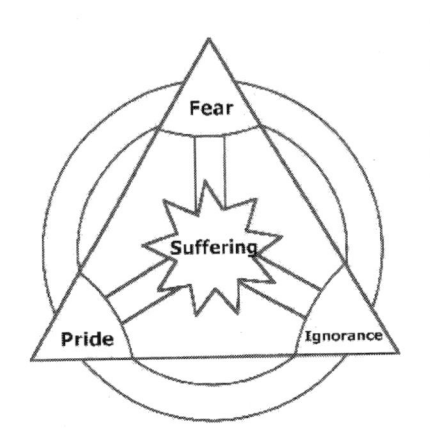

Fear: The irrational aversion to what can be helpful

Pride: A rigid identity that does not allow for change or adaptability.

Ignorance: The reliance on simplistic thinking to avoid complex understanding.

Be advised to not think of these three words as you might normally. What the trinity of suffering does is provide excuses, and you are to live a life without excuses.

Fear, Pride and Ignorance provide excuses for not going after your destiny.

Fear

A person who acts with a sense of destiny does not allow fear to prevent him or her from doing what will help them. While a person of destiny may not enjoy a visit to the doctor, if a long and active life is part of their destiny then they will not hesitate. Saving money for some may be an annoying effort, but that won't stop someone who is destined for wealth.

Building Your Cult

Pride

To be hindered by pride simply means that you see yourself in a certain light, and that perspective prevents you from changing. You can hear this in the words, "that's how I've always been. I can't change."

Destiny should be your only constant – your polar star. Everything else, including yourself, must be subject to change. It is the only way to navigate a world that does the unexpected.

Ignorance

Ignorance means relying on false reasoning processes. What follows is only a partial list of these false reasoning processes:

Minimizing: Trying to make the offense seem small.

> "I only stabbed him once."

Justifying: Avoiding responsibility for behavior, a person finds a reason for their actions.

> "He yelled at me so I had to hit him."
> "They all did it so why can't I?"

Excuse Making: Creating a context where the action might appear more reasonable.

> "I was drunk when I set my friend on fire."

Blaming: To avoid accepting responsibility a scapegoat is created.

> "The principal had is out for me. That's why I got expelled."

Building Your Cult

Victimstance: When a person is held accountable for their behavior they will portray themself as the victim. They act as though the world is against them. When playing the victim the person does not take responsibility for changing any behaviors, as they believe they are helpless to do so.

> *"These assignments are too hard for me."*
> *"I can't play football because therapy sessions are during practice."*

The Trinity of Suffering is presented to you to remind you that if you are a person of destiny then you will not yield to excuses.

The World

You have a relationship with yourself and you have a relationship with the World. These two relationships also must be in balance. To be too focused on yourself is to isolate yourself from others in hopes to better "wrestle with your demons" in order to one day emerge a whole and ready person (a day which seldom comes). To be too focused on the World leaves you living without a good examination of your life, and as Socrates said, "an unexamined life is not worth living."

The World is the crucible in which you test all you have learned. The World is the theater in which you make your Destiny unfold. Your Destiny and your great Plan is the script that will guide you.

Because The World is filled with people who each have their own ambitions you must enter the realm of politics. Politics is, simply put, the science and art of protecting and promoting your own interests.

Within The World there are things over which you have much control and which can serve to help fulfill your destiny.

Propaganda

Propaganda is the art of giving information to others that presents you and your cult in the best possible light. Propaganda is not about being completely honest, so fact and fiction are often mixed to weave a tale that is always favorable.

Building Your Cult

To create an effective propaganda campaign the easiest way is to link images of people with certain valuable traits to a symbol.

Consider any popular television commercial like Nike and it's popular "swoosh" symbol that is at the end of every commercial. Consider the famous Coke-Cola commercial with people singing "I'd like to teach the world to sing." Likewise, political commercials are often more overt with slogan like, "Trusted. Reliable. Bob Smith for Senate."

Personal Propaganda And Image

Personal Propaganda is about how you want to present yourself to the world. This is something on which politicians spend endless amounts of time. The same should be true for you as a cult

Building Your Cult

leader.

    This can be very difficult because the message you want to portray should be consistent over time (that is until you need to change it). The difficulty of maintaining a suitable image is that it takes constant awareness.

Here are a few examples of lapses in awareness:

- The starlet who exits the car at the wrong time to reveal her nickers, or lack thereof to the flashing cameras of the paparazzi (if not intentional).
- The morally upright religious leader who has his indiscretions with prostitutes printed all over the paper.
- The business man who forgot how having sex with employees could come back to haunt him.

    The most straightforward solution to this problem is to do a variation of what people do in Alcoholics Anonymous and perform a "fearless moral inventory." In doing so you will uncover all the parts of your character that could be seen by others as failings or lapses in character and spin them so they are a positive part of your image. These will be parts of your character that you don't want to alter that have given you reward and pleasure. A few people who have done this quite successfully are Hugh Hefner, who pursues young women without apology to be his girlfriends and courtesans, and let's not forget Donald Trump who has come to personify egomania and greed.

    Part of your personal presentation is what you wear. Many religious cult leaders will don strange attire to maintain an other worldly appearance. Some will wear clothes that seem from another culture or be seen only wearing a solid color.

    It is also a good idea to have a presentation that attracts people. This can be done by behaving in a way that demonstrates

Building Your Cult

confidence and magnanimity.

By combining all of these together you will create what many refer to as an "Avatar." An Avatar is a character whose looks and behaviors help evoke specific feelings in others. You can also think of an avatar as a personification of your ideal. So if you want to be the leader that attracts people to work for you then this is your chance to explore that type of personality.

If you are interested in gaining a romantic partner it's a good idea to be specific. Do you want to attract sex partners or an ideal mate? Think carefully, because there is a difference.

To create that avatar you must return to your personal values and ideals. Begin to envision the person who would best personify those ideals and then build yourself into that person. If you want to become someone different than what you are now then the change must be drastic. You can completely reinvent yourself.

The danger of this degree of reinvention is that there will likely be remnants of your former self still in play.

The solution to this is not to eradicate these other part of you but to simply place them aside and consider them to be "useful at another time." This prevents you from treating any part of your personality as an enemy, and you will find that every part of your personalty has it's place.

By creating an avatar you are exercising your ability to learn new skills and becoming more flexible to the situations around you.

Over time you will discover that the avatar you created is in fact YOU. In reality it has always been you. It was simply a "you" that you had not been familiar with. Eventually the avatar will integrate into your personality and find it's place so that it will be there for you when you need it.

Other Forms Of Personal Propaganda

Another form of personal propaganda is hearsay and rumor. Nothing can more quickly build or destroy a person's reputation than

Building Your Cult

a widespread and unsubstantiated rumor. Knowing this, it is always best to create the rumors that you want spread about you before anyone else does.

It will be more effective if you appear to have no direct connection to your rumor campaign. You can start an effective rumor campaign with one person, a friend, who can spread the rumor for you and you can do the same in exchange. This person is often referred to as a wingman, and from one wingman you can build an entourage. A wingman is a person who is there to make you look good and create positive and compelling rumors about your reputation.

I once used a wingman to promote me as psychic at a social function. He would introduce me as his friend "the psychic". At the end of the evening I had a line of people asking for help in the form of my psychic skills. His efforts sealed my reputation for the people I met. *(You can read more about that in my book **The Handbook Of Psychic Cold Reading,** available through online retailers and bookstores.)*

Building an entourage can also dramatically improve your image and reputation. An entourage is a small group of people that surround you to make you look important. An entourage does not have to be big to do the job, three to six people is enough.

When employing an entourage it's best to use it where it will make the biggest impact, usually large public events where you will be seen by a lot of people: conventions, seminars, grand openings and movie premiers are good examples. Your entourage will make them wonder why you have such a following.

There are several ways to get an entourage. The simplest way is to ask friends to become part of your entourage. Ensure that they

Building Your Cult

will have a fun time doing it and pay them if you think you need to. Make sure that everyone knows their role before hand. The roles within your entourage could be manager, bodyguards, girlfriends, photographer, biographer or just ordinary fans and sycophants. Make sure they play their role to the hilt ... and to the public.

Be certain that when asked who they are that your entourage members respond with your name, as in *"I'm part of Dantalion Jones' group."* By doing this they will be spreading your name and your clout. They should also be friendly and welcoming, as this is also a part of making you look good.

To understand the power of an entourage consider how some movie stars are made to look more important by having two husky bodyguards and two beautiful women accompanying them. They will always get more attention on the red carpet than the movie star who shows up with just their date.

Live Efficiently

Living efficiently means being aware of your energy and not wasting it on things that distract you from your destiny. This is a bigger responsibility than you might think because it means choosing efficient responses to life's diverse events. Consider that anger is a common response to unexpected situations, but anger is seldom an efficient reaction and it often distracts you from your destiny.

Choosing to not get angry is much harder than you might think, but is a skill that will be more useful than you can imagine.

If your goals and ambitions require other people then you must enter the realm of politics where people will maneuver for their own ambitions and sometimes do so at your expense.

Part of living efficiently is being aware that people have ambitions of their own, and their ambitions may run counter to your own. Keep secret as much as possible your own ambitions and sense of destiny. Yes, they say "You're only as sick as your secrets" so the key is to keep your secrets as healthy and supportive of your ambitions as possible.

One of the most efficient cults around, Scientology, has efficiency incorporated into its culture. They have made a point of measuring **everything** in order to find ways of making even the smallest improvement in how their cult functions. For Scientology a change that makes a 4% profit increase is implemented just as quickly as one that makes an 80% increase.

Fulfilling Peoples Needs

If you are to be an icon of influence (whether or not that means leading your own cult) understanding the nature of human needs is vital. As a human being you yourself are not unaffected by them so understanding human needs means understanding yourself and others.

Understand, that reading about human needs is not enough. To deeply understand the affect that human needs have on our lives requires endless meditation and observation. You must must observe how these needs move and influence you first to understand their power. Only after some time of doing this personal observation may you become humble enough to see the depth these needs drive others.

When you recognize how you can fulfill the needs of others they will eagerly want to follow your lead.

What follows are two types of human needs. The first describes needs that act as core motivations in life. The second list of needs applies within our interacting with others.

The 5 Cental Human Needs

There are five human needs that will help you in two ways.

Building Your Cult

First by understanding these needs you will better understand yourself and your own motivations and secondly it will help you understand what motivates other people to make decisions.

When you recognize these needs in others and offer to fulfill them you'll find them eager to follow you. One can witness these needs in action simply by noticing the decisions people make.

Like all types of human needs they all coexist and vary in intensity through time. We'll explore each of these needs in detail. They are Security, Freedom, Belonging, Competence and Creativity.

Security

Security fulfills a persons need to be safe. This need can be an intense need with people who have volitile childhoods and people who suffer from anxiety disorders. This is also true of people who have recently experienced times of chaos and uncertainty. Uncertainty in people can create a compensatory need for safety.

People with strong needs for security are often willing to give up certain freedoms, and even sacrifice the freedoms of others in order to maintain the feeling of security. A good example of this is how some people felt that martial law was justifiable to keep themselves safe from the chaos and uncertainty of terrorism.

For people who value Security you can use these key phrases "relax", "safe", "put yourself at ease", "secure", "take a step back", "you're safe".

Freedom

Freedom allows people to not feel controlled. Those who highly value Freedom are often willing to sacrifice a degree of security to maintain their security. Freedom and Security tend to have a reciprical relationship. The greater need for Security the lesser the need for Freedom and vise versa.

People with a strong need for Freedom may well be

adventure seekers and willing to step into danger just for the thrill of it.

When you recognize a persons need for freedom you can use these key phrases "Not be tied down", "No limitations", "complete freedom", "limitless" and "not be held back".

Belonging

The need to belong is of great appeal to a cult members. Belonging to a unique group permits a person to be special.

Belonging is a central reason people join and stay in churches, cults, gangs and the reason people stay in jobs even if their other needs are not fulfilled. People with a strong need to belong will often be willing to limit themselves to be a part of the group. They may also seek to be led.

Creativity

Creativity is a need that helps an individual express their uniqueness.

Just as Freedom and Security have a reciprical relationship with each other Belonging and Creativity have a loosely reciprical relationship.

People can exercise Creativity when the have a high need for Belonging however many people with a strong need to Belong tend to value it at the expence of creative self expression and often look for guidance instead of seek self expression.

Competence

Competence is the need to know that are good at something.

Consider a time when you got a new job and you wanted to know you were doing the right thing **and** be acknowledged for it.

Like most human needs these are not static. A needs intencity will wax and wane as life progresses. When one need is fulfilled to the complete satisfaction of the individual they will very likely focus on satisfying one of the other needs.

What you will notice is that people often have personalities that are built around the promaneces and deficency of these needs and one or two of these needs will remain a constant influence throughout their life.

As an example a person who values creativity will build their life about being "unique". You might recognize them as often wearing dark clothes and purple hair. At their best they are wonderful artists. At their worst they feel isolated and look at themselves as strangers in a foreign land.

Someone with a strong need for security and belonging will often wrap themselves within corporate culture. Then know that as long as they are part of the larger organization they will not have to worry about what to do next. The company will take care of them.

The Seven Relationship Needs

The Seven relationship needs were first described by author Blair Warren in his book "The Forbidden Keys to Persuasion" and refered to as "The 7 Hidden Addictions".

The Seven relationship needs are things that everyone reponds to in some positive way. Therefor in ever interaction is you will benefit when you fulfill as many of them as possible. They are as follows:

- **The need to feel in control.**

Feeling in control is not about being a control freak and micromanaging every personal interchange. Feeling in control is about feeling as if you have a choice.

Building Your Cult

- **The need to be needed.**

This relationship need is about feeling a sense of importance within the relationship.

- **The need for hope during challenges.**

When someone feels stuck in an uncomfortable situation they will do anything to feel some sense of hope. Offer them hope and they will love you but be sure you can help them.

- **The need for a scape goat.**

As much as we preach personal responcibility there is no greater releaf than being told "It's not your fault." This is because of the intense discomfort that comes from having to re-evaluate the beliefs we have about ourselves.

- **The need to be noticed and feel understood.**

There is a very positive and wonderful feeling that we all feel when we are with someone who seems to *truly* understand us. On the other hand when you are asked to defend yourslf point of view or actions you certainly do not feel understood. To truly master applying this need means to always be aware of your questioning so to never make someone feel defencive.

- **The need to know things they shoudn't know.**

Everyone wants to know secrets. When someone is given an opportunity to know a secret they feel special. To put this need into action one does not have to say "I've got a secret." instead all they have to do is *imply* they have a secret.

- **The need to be right.**

Just like the need to be noticed and understood, when you fulfill someones need to be right they are powerfully affected. It is

Building Your Cult

the exact opposite feeling of defenciveness, it's a complete total affirmation.

Creating The Organization To Fulfill Your Ambitions

When the time becomes right and more people are needed to help you achieve your goals and destiny you can begin to focus on creating a group of people (a cult) that will function as your proxy.

For any organization you choose to create it needs to incorporate your values throughout every level. This can be done by making these values an overt part of the cult structure and developing processes that refocus attention towards those values.

You can begin by finding people who share your goals, or at least whose goals are in line with your goals and ambitions. There are two ways to do this. The first is through conversation, but be aware that people will often say anything to make you believe they are on your side. The other method is more subtle and certain – observation.

By patiently observing them they will demonstrate their values and beliefs. It is then that you can begin to funnel them into your cult and offer them incentives and bribes that will make them feel welcomed and motivated.

Work hard to find out what truly motivates each person. While some people will do great things for a bonus someone else will work just as hard for praise and recognition.

As you uncover the values and motivations of the people in your cult remember your goal is to create motivated clones of yourself that want the same outcomes as you, and would typically do things in the way you would do them. The best way of doing this is to slowly, secretly test them and observe how they perform.

Remind each individual that they are part of a great mission and their special talent is vital for its completion. Their job with you, whether window washer or CPA, is part of a great and divine plan. Never let them forget it.

Building Your Cult

You can help them remember this mission in both obvious and subtle ways. The obvious ways can be done at group meetings where they restate the cult mission. Subtle tactics include incorporating cult symbolism at every level, from logos on letterheads to group uniforms and cult jewelry.

Recap Of Doctrine

- **The One Person:** You, The Individual are the central figure and power in your life. Like it or not, your life is within your control. There is no guilt, no shame and no excuses.
- **The Two Promises To Remember:** The Promise to remember you are loved and the promise to remember you have a destiny.
- **The Three Internal Forces:** Thinking, Feeling and Doing
- **The Many:** All the "parts" of you, your wants, needs, habits and desires.
- **Your Destiny:** You are the central figure around which great things will happen. That is your destiny.
- **Create A Mythos**: Write and tell stories that glorify your life and your efforts. They do not have to be "true." They can pass as being "true enough."
- **The World:** The world will help you accomplish your goals.
- **Propaganda:** Propaganda is the art of giving information that presents you to the world in the best possible light. Use it for yourself and your cult.
- **Your Cult:** Your cult is the organization you form that will help you accomplish your goals and your destiny.
- The Trinity of Suffering: Fear, Pride and Ignorance.

Note how each part of the Doctrine can be expounded upon in greater detail.

www.BuildingYourCult.com

Building Your Cult

Build Your Own Personal Doctrine

The doctrine given you is just an example. You are welcome to use it as you see fit.

Consider what you would have as your own personal doctrine. One that would best help you build the life you most desire and make it your own.

Begin with the values that are most important to you and rules of thumb by which you would eagerly live. Write them down first in simple phrases and then later build on them by turning them into essays.

Last Piece of Advice: Learn Hypnosis

You don't have to learn hypnosis and most effective cult leaders don't know a darned thing about it. Those that do, use it very very effectively.

Before you rush out and buy all sorts of hypnosis books and courses there are a few things that you should know about the subject.

In the world of hypnosis there are two types of hypnosis, they are called *covert* and *authoritarian* hypnosis. Before getting into a description of their pros and cons let me tell you how they differ.

Authoritarian hypnosis is the type of hypnosis process that most people are familiar with. It consists of one person being the hypnotist and another being the hypnosis subject. The hypnotist overtly tells the subject what to do by giving them clear instructions to follow.

Authoritarian hypnosis is the process used in most hypnotherapy and stage hypnosis shows.

Covert hypnosis, on the other hand, is more "sneaky" and can be done without the subject actually knowing the process is taking place. Under the umbrella of covert hypnosis falls the field of Neuro Linguistic Programming (NLP for short) which has been co-oped

Building Your Cult

into various sales trainings and "rapid romance" trainings.

Each form of hypnosis has it's benefits. Covert hypnosis is wonderful for sales training and wooing people into a sincere feeling of friendship.

For a cult leader who wants to use authoritarian hypnosis it can be done by hiding it within the guise of "guided meditation" or "imagination exercise".

Be prepared to discover that the most value you will get from learning hypnosis is when you use it on yourself.

I've written about both these forms of hypnosis. For authoritarian hypnosis you can read **Mind Control Hypnosis** and covert forms of hypnosis are described in **Mind Control Language Patterns**. Both of these are available at online book sellers or from www.MindControlPublishing.com.

Building Your Cult

A Story

As mentioned in this book, your life is a saga, and to that end I wrote this short but epic story for you to consider. This story originally appeared in "The Forbidden Book Of Getting What You Want."

Here is a story you would be wise to read, about an errant God who was cast to earth.

This God had committed a great transgression and was punished by his fellow Gods, condemned to live imprisoned in a mortal human body.

At his birth he was trapped inside an infant body with only an infant's ability to move and speak. As he grew, every outward aspect of his life seemed ordinary, except that he knew inside he was a God. He knew that in spite of his appearance, his family and his upbringing, there was nothing ordinary about him.

He decided that if he could not reclaim the greatness of a God then he would build his greatness as a man.

Every action he took moved him in that direction. He did so with a calm and undisturbed patience, for he knew that inside he was a God.

All the time he kept silent about who he knew he really was. To speak of it would only cause others to think him mad and egocentric. As he grew he accomplished one thing after another. Some people praised him, but it meant nothing to him. Others were envious and threatened by his achievements, but he was unmoved.

He continued to live a life of achievement.

On his death bed, he was surrounded by his friends and associates. Their eyes were filled with tears as they saw life slowly passing from him.

One of his closest friends leaned forward and asked, "you have done so much for all of us and for yourself. How can we

Building Your Cult

possibly live up to your achievements?" And in that moment he saw something in everyone around him that he had never recognized before. He saw a light within each of them that was the light of his former life as a god.

Still holding on to his secret and knowing that his imprisonment was about to end his last words were uttered: "Take what is important and live it."

As the light from his human eyes faded his real eyes opened, surrounded by the gods who had condemned him. Smiles filled their faces and they welcomed his return as if he were a returning king. Without them ever telling him, he knew then his sentence was not a punishment but a blessing given by his closest friends.

APPENDIX

Building Your Cult

Unleash the Addict

Who am I?

My name is Dantalion Jones. That's not my real, name but it's real enough for now.

The origin of my interest in the mind came at a young age when I first witnessed a stage hypnotist at the county fair. Since that time my interest has never ceased.

For a huge part of my professional life I've worked as a hypnotist, NLP practitioner, and seminar leader. I figure I've worked with more than 3000 people doing over 9,000 hours of hypnosis and NLP. Out of my experience I've written several books on hypnosis and mind control...and I never get tired of testing the limits of what can be done. I wanted to test all the claims:

Could life long phobias be eliminated in 10 minutes?
Could smoking habits be eliminated in one session?
Can a couch potato be turned into an exercise addict?

I've discovered that with a little good instruction and fearless attitude it's possible to test how people can be controlled to respond.

My first tests were to simply see if I could hypnotize people. In my youth I had plenty of volunteers and I discovered that yes, I could hypnotize people. I found that hypnosis was rather easy.

Youth followed into adolescence and my awareness turned to a combination of raging hormones and lustful frustration. Could I apply my knowledge of the mind to seduction? Yes, I could and that strong motivation showed me the value of adapting to

Building Your Cult

circumstances.

I've also allowed myself to see how far I can be influenced and manipulated, and that is what impressed me the most. I found that there are actions that people can take and, if well executed, I was at their mercy no matter how hard I might try.

What all this theory and testing has revealed to me is that in spite our best efforts we can, in fact, be influenced and manipulated against our will. It's a tricky maneuver, but it can be done.

In the pages that follow I'm going to cover the issue of addiction. What are the mental components that make up an addiction? Can they be manipulated? Can addictions be created and destroyed at will? If so then how?

Of course, I ask that you use this information with great caution, and you will find warnings to that effect throughout this document.

Dantalion Jones

What is "Unleash The Addict"?

Here you will be given the following information based on my own experience and testing:

- You will understand the concept of addiction. This is based on my own experience, so some aspects of it may fly in the face of commonly accepted psychology.

- You will learn about the most basic human motivations and drives, and how to connect with them so that people are called into action.

- You will learn how to elicit an addictive feeling and link it to anything you want. This is akin to being able to create an addiction in anyone.

Why Teach "Unleash The Addict"?

At first glance (and perhaps second and third) teaching someone how to create an addiction in another person may seem downright wicked. For that reason I'll give you my list of reasons why I'm teaching "Unleash the Addict."

I Am Not The Information Police

Yes, I want this information to be used wisely and with kindness, but it's not my job to police who receives this knowledge. If you paid for it you deserve to have it. I just ask that you use it wisely and do everything you can to monitor yourself.

Building Your Cult

People Want To Know If This Is Possible

The ability to control people's thoughts has been alluded to in a lot of different areas. The US Government created the covert program MK ULTRA during the Cold War where they studied how to control people by all sorts of unsavory means.

In the mid 1970's the field of Neuro Linguistic Programming (NLP) came about with wild claims of being able to program people to create and remove phobias, as well as free people from unwanted habits. NLP quickly move to the forefront of the brief therapy movement. It also became suspect as a tool for cult recruitment.

NLP later entered into the world of seduction and further implied that the human will is weaker than we might have hoped.

People Want To Know How To Do It

People have an innate interest in human manipulation. Their interest may be from a fear of being manipulated themselves or from an adolescent desire for power and control over others, or a combination of both. Either way, it is a "sexy" topic and people want to know.

Thankfully, most people will not use this information for ill. They are curious. The good news is that by learning how this process is done you are also learning how the mind works, and that can benefit you in all sorts of areas of life.

People Want To Know How To Undo An Addiction

That's right. As much as you can learn to make an addiction you can also reverse the process and **undo** the addiction. Keep in mind that people are different and some are more susceptible to addiction than others.

Building Your Cult

People Want To Protect Themselves From Manipulation

Knowledge is power. Knowing how addictions can be created in people gives you the ability to detect if it were ever used on you. By knowing what you are learning here you are protecting yourself and will be aware when it happens.

People Want To Be Able To Do This To Themselves

The one benefit to learning how to create addictions is that you can create them within yourself and do it with control. Doing this to yourself prevents you from going out of control because you will also know how to undo what you've done to yourself.

How would your life be different if you were addicted to learning and practicing a new skill? Perhaps you are an athlete and you want to be addicted to a training regimen. Or perhaps you want to build a financial empire within the next five years? Would an addiction be of use, if you could keep it under control?

People Want To Coach Others For Fitness Addiction

I have to admit that this is not always a good thing, but you'll find people who want it and are willing to pay coaches and therapists to help them become addicted. They want to be addicted to good grades, athletic fitness, health and beneficial activity. I know. I have had more than a few of these people as clients.

People Want To Do It To Other People

Yeah, it's true. People have less than benevolent intentions, but I'm not here to enforce good behavior. I can only encourage it.

Before you jump on the book burning bandwagon to destroy this book and limit your own First Amendment protections I would like to point out what I've learned about people. My first observation

www.BuildingYourCult.com

is that there are people who want to use these tools with malicious intent, but there are several factors that tend to decrease their success. One factor is that it takes a lot of skill to apply these concepts with any effectiveness. By the time a person has gained enough skill at doing a malicious process to someone their interest has usually waned. One reason is that they've had to learn about these processes by applying them on themselves. This usually creates a sense of empathy, and takes all the fun out of doing malicious things to people.

Another reason they tend not to apply these skills maliciously is a sneaky benefit of learning them. It's like a sneaky magic trick where you want one thing but you get something better instead. The "instead" comes when a person starts to realize what their own motivations are in life, and they tend to no longer want to mess with other people's heads. After studying these processes and uncovering one's own motivation, revenge and manipulation thankfully becomes a memory.

So relax. There are good things that come from learning how to create addictions.

My Understanding Of Addictions

Yes, I've worked with addicts in all sorts of ways. But I think the turning point came when I got into a conversation with a co-worker who talked to me about being a recovering alcoholic. I had to admit to her that I don't completely understand addiction, and so I asked her to describe what **her** experience of addiction was like.

She began to explain the mania and craziness that happened to her when she drank and how fun it was to be in that tornado of mania. She then explained how the next day introduced her to the frightening disaster her whirlwind had wrought. Upon realizing what

Building Your Cult

she had done she found herself torn between the uncertainty of sobriety and the secure escapism of drinking.

This described **her** version of addiction. I'm sure there are others.

For another friend, also an alcoholic, his addiction to alcohol was a way of gaining control over his depression. He explained that while it didn't work very well, it did give him a feeling of control.

As a general rule most people with addictions tend to be fairly nice people when they are not being ruled by their addiction. This is because they have been able to compartmentalize their addiction and keep it separate from the rest of their life – the alcoholic mom who only drinks when everyone has gone to sleep or the sex addict who has a secret room to hide his fetish material.

The point is that while addiction can be reduced to a mental process that can be explained in a book, each person has their own unique mental process for addiction, so be aware and be flexible to people and to circumstances.

Continuing onward, the next section is going to deal with your own mental processes. It will focus on what you think about your own abilities.

Building Your Cult

Confidence

For lack of a better term you are going to become a "conman."

That is, you are to become a conman in all the **GOOD** definitions of the word. By that I mean that to do anything as bold and daring as creating an addiction in someone you have to...have to...**YOU MUST**...have a confidence that you can do it. It doesn't matter if you are only doing it for the first time, you must act and breathe as if you have done it 1,000 times with great results.

Interestingly, if you had that sense of confidence and never finished reading this book and went out to create addictions in people you would be completely surprised how successful you would be. Granted, you would have plenty of false starts and failures, but if you **KNEW** you could do it you would eventually discover how it could be done.

The reasoning behind that is one of flexibility. If you knew it could be done and that you could do it then you would be completely flexible.

You will notice that very confident people usually have lots of people around them. This is because confidence make people feel safe, and they want to bask in a feeling of security. Your own sense of confidence is infectious, and having it gives other people a sense of confidence in their own abilities. All the better reason to start demonstrating confidence in your own ability.

To get that confidence you must avoid the trap of "needing more information." This is what many people do when they start to

Building Your Cult

learn a new skill. They convince themselves that they can do it, but only when they know everything about it. They go about hording information and knowledge but never go out to test it. They want to do it perfectly the first time, but fear the wonderful lessons they can learn by falling on their face and having fun with it.

This is just as true with any skill of persuasion or influence (or any skill in general). So, as you read this book and mentally process the instructions create a feeling of certainty that you can do it. In fact, don't wait for further instructions. Put aside every doubt, and upon reading how something is done you can mentally see, hear and feel yourself doing it perfectly. Do this repeatedly and you will find your skill level in all areas of your life begin to skyrocket.

www.BuildingYourCult.com

Building Your Cult

Getting Into People's Minds And The Need For Rapport

Rapport is one of those things that everyone who teaches influence, persuasion and interrogation makes a big deal about...even me.

To understand rapport try to think of what it's like when people get "in sync" with each other, like two dancers that have practiced with each other so much that they can "read" their partner. Rapport happens for the rest of us when we begin to feel comfortable and connected to the other person. In those moments anything becomes possible: criminals confess, people fall in love, and sales are made. It is also with rapport that one can more effectively use the skills to create an addiction. So it behooves us to learn how to create rapport and use it to our advantage.

To learn rapport it is good to keep in mind that it's a two way street. It's not really something you **do** to someone, as much as it's a feeling your **share** with them. Rapport, thus, is one reason that it can be difficult to do wicked things to people: it often has a boomerang effect on the user. That's good to keep in mind when you consider creating a malicious addiction within someone.

That said, let's explain some ways to build rapport.

Ways To Build Rapport

When I first began to study the mind and Neuro Linguistic Programming in particular there was a strong, almost obsessive, emphasis on rapport techniques. The reason why is that it became clear that rapport was the doorway that enters into that inner sanctum of influence.

Building Your Cult

"With rapport anything is possible. Without it nothing is possible" was the mantra. So the first part of every NLP training focused on rapport. These exercises were based on behaviors that happen *after* rapport is created, behaviors called "mirroring and matching."

Mirroring and matching is about putting your body posture and position into the same posture as the person with whom you want rapport. This is not the same as "monkey see monkey do," because that is too obvious. Instead, the person who wants to build rapport waits about ten seconds before positioning themselves like the other person. Ten seconds is enough time to not look obvious about what you're doing.

This exercise of "mirroring and matching" strangely worked to build rapport...and it' is still taught today. The only possible drawback is that for people new to doing this exercise it tends to feel forced, contrived and awkward. It does take some practice to get used to.

What many NLPers have overlooked is that this mirroring and matching behavior is much more a **result** of rapport than a cause of it. It is much like putting the cart before the horse...it works, but it's cumbersome.

It's therefore best to **start** with rapport. But how?

The answer is simple and elegant: **assume** you are already it rapport!

If you're asking "how do I assume I already have rapport?" then I'll tell you. Remember that rapport is a state that is often described by a sense of liking and connection to someone. If you are to assume you have rapport with someone then create a feeling of

www.BuildingYourCult.com

Building Your Cult

liking toward that person. Imagine you are long time friends who have much in common. You have to **feel** a connection with them, like you were already old friends.

As I mentioned before, rapport of this nature can make it difficult to do something wicked and malicious to someone, so consider that a good thing.

You can, however, use it to help and benefit them. Perhaps they want to be more fit or be a better student. You could show them how to become addicted to exercise or studying.

So start by assuming you have rapport with the other person. If you are new to this skill then practice it with everyone you meet, and notice how easily they open up and how comfortable it can become for both of you.

Pacing And Dragging

"Pacing and dragging" is term I heard that is a play on the NLP phrase "pacing and leading." Pacing and leading is when you begin to follow what someone else is doing, and then gradually you take the lead and they begin to follow you. This is done in racing as you might guess, but it is also done in conversations where you agree with what the person said, add a comment, then turn the conversation more to the direction you want. Suffice it to say that pacing and leading can be done in **any** interaction where two or more people are involved.

Pacing and Dragging has bit more energy to it than pacing and leading. Pacing and dragging is akin to being pulled along by someone's force, enthusiasm, confidence and conviction. Maybe you've experienced it yourself. You're with someone who gives you *all* of their attention and guides and leads you through some amazing experience. Maybe it's just a story they are telling...or maybe they talked you into a bungee jump, but somehow you got "captured" by all the energy and excitement they exuded. That is what pacing and dragging feels like, and while you're in it it can be a wonderful ride.

In the next section the model of addiction is going to be dissected and described in terms of an impulse of "pull."

The Two Types Of Pull

I use the word "pull" to describe addictions because a pull is something that is an external force that is not always within the control of the person being pulled. If you talk to people about their addictions you will hear how they are not in control and that they feel "pulled" to act on the addiction. They are often torn by the fact that they know they **should** have it under control, but don't.

There are many types of "pulls" that people have to deal with every day, and not all of them are addictions. They range from the mild preference to the "gotta have chocolate" desire, but for the sake of the topic of addictions let's talk about the most power "pulls" that drive us.

The Compelling Pull

The compelling pull tends to drive our lives in sometimes invisible ways. A compelling pull is best described by the values that motivate us. While all of us have values, we don't always know what they are, and quite often our values are so poorly defined that we find ourselves torn about what to do.

Values, when clear, make decisions easy. For example, a salesman is closing a big sale and he receives a call telling him his car is being towed away. At that moment he is faced with a decision. If he values for his car more than the sale he leaves the sale to get his

Building Your Cult

car. On the other hand, if the business deal is more important, he closes the deal and then deals with his missing car later.

Getting to someone's compelling pull is very easy because it is based on what is important to them, and people love to talk about what is important to them. Why? Because it's important to them!

So to get to know someone's compelling pull all you have to do is ask them what's important. You can ask them what is important to them in life if you want to get to their life goals and life motives, but if you want to influence them in specific areas then you have to ask them what is important in those specific areas. For example, if you want to find a person's compelling pull regarding lovers then you would simply ask them, "what's important to you in a lover?" and then listen very carefully.

But beware, their first answer is only the surface answer, and you must go further to reach what pulls them compellingly towards a lover. For their first answer they may tell you "trust," or maybe they'll say "kindness" or "attractiveness." Every person is different. You're not done. In fact you've just started. If you stop there it is unlikely that you will get very far at all...there will be no "pull," because their first answer is largely intellectual and not emotional.

You will then respond to their response with agreement, remembering how rapport is vital to the process, and then ask a related but similar question "What's important to you about 'trust'?" or kindness or attractiveness...whatever they told you. From that you will get another answer that takes you closer still to their compelling pull. So they may say, "what's important about 'trust' is it gives me security" Whatever they answer you will agree, like before, perhaps talking about it, and then repeating the process again.

Usually, this process of asking, "what's important about...?"

Building Your Cult

will take place three or more times. You will know when you've reached their compelling pull when you notice a strong emotional response. The person will "light up" when then reach the truest and deepest responses.

Okay, let's stop for a moment.

Remember when we talking about about imagining what it would be like to be the other person during the discussion of rapport? If you've practiced it you'll get very good at noticing when they have their emotional response, but pay attention. This is something that you may not notice if you were simply engaging in a normal conversation.

To get good at this it's important to practice finding people's compelling pull in different contexts and with different people. Find out what's important to them about "lover," "romance," "a car," "learning," etc. and notice what their compelling pull might be. It could be "excitement," or "peace of mind," What you'll notice is that their pull is likely an abstract idea, feeling or concept that has great meaning to them.

So what next?

First you'll need to recognize what the process has accomplished already. It's assumed you have begun with your rapport skills. Because you focused on them and what they value you will find that your rapport with them has increased. Also, it is very likely that, at some level, they have already begun a process of linking good feelings to you.

Your second step is another process that can be even more powerful for both you and your subject. This is where you take their value, their pull, and apply it wherever you want. The secret is to

Building Your Cult

apply it to a specific context. So, if you wanted to find out their compelling pull in a lover (wink) and you began the process by asking them "what's important in lover?" and you went through the entire process of finding the pull for them...you **could** link that word to yourself.

To do that you might say something like, *"when I think of (name their compelling pull) I know that's important to me too in a lover...and I feel those feelings too."*

This can be done for any context, but you have to apply it to the context to which you first applied it. Asking, "what is important to you in a car?" and find out their compelling pull it will be of little use if you connect that pull to their idea of a lover.

At the risk of oversimplifying the process here it is broken down step by step:

Step 1 – Build Rapport
Do this by using the classic NLP "mirror and matching" exercises, as well as assuming you already have rapport and the "stepping into their body" technique mentioned earlier.

Step 2 – Elicit The Pull
Determine the context in which you want to influence them and ask them "what's important about...?"

Step 3 – Continue To Elicit Until You Reach Feelings
Whatever they say, agree with them and then ask, "what is important about that thing." You may have to ask this several times until you get a strong emotional response. If you go too far you'll get anger and frustration from them, so practice doing this in a conversational manner and with varying phraseology. Note what word or phrase creates a strong emotional response with them and use it in the next

step.

Step 4 – Link What Pulls Them To You In The Right Context
Use the "pull" which they gave you and link it in words and behaviors to you or your product or service.

It's important to note that a compelling pull is not the same as an addictive pull. The difference between the two is one of intensity and need for repeated behaviors.

The compelling pull is usually more than enough to get someone to take action, and this can certainly be used on yourself with great effectiveness. In fact, just as you should with any technique such as this, it's a good idea to apply it to yourself before doing it with someone else. Doing so will heighten your awareness as to what it might feel like for another person. It might also make you more compassionate (and resistant) about using this process in a harmful way.

Statement Of Responsible Use

Before continuing on into the topic of addiction it should be noted that some people are more susceptible to addictions than others. Some people have such a natural tendency for addiction that you may create one without intending to. For reasons I'll call "responsible use" I would like to go into why it's best to avoid creating addictions in these types of people when you recognize them.

Please realize that what I'm going to explain may completely turn you off to creating addictions. If so it's a sign you likely have a good conscience and have compassion toward others. Good for you! But like I have said earlier, I am not the information police, so here goes.

Building Your Cult

The most powerful level of addiction comes from a very deep sense of loss. Not the type of loss when you lose $20. Not the type of loss when you flunk a class. Not even the type of loss when your car gets totaled. The deep sense of loss that forms the most addictive personalities can best be described as "childhood abandonment." This is the type of intense loss that happens at such an early age that it helps form how someone thinks of themselves. In a word, they think of themselves as "empty." Feeling empty inside, they will hang on to anything that will either give them some sense of completeness or help them forget the emptiness. When they have it they are satisfied, but only for a moment and that moment passes. When it does the emptiness is there again. The cycle is ripe for repeating itself. Their addiction could be for anything, drugs, sex, love, food, exercise, success. The list is endless.

Do you **really** want to create an addiction with this type of person? If you hesitated to answer that, then let me continue with why you should avoid them.

The first reason is one of simple ethics: it's not nice. Don't be the type of person who increases the suffering of people who are already suffering. The golden rule is not a law but it's a rule that works pretty well.

The second reason is legal. If you are in a position of authority to counsel someone – priest, teacher, hypnotist, psychologist, doctor, etc. – then you have what the law describes as a *in loco parentus* responsibility to your clients. Literally *in loco parentus* means "in the place of the parent," and sets forth that your professional behavior is to be in the best interest of the client. If it is not, you could find yourself on some very shaky ground.

The third reason is rational: you won't like the results you

Building Your Cult

get. If you work with one of these addictive personalities to create an addiction then it is a good idea to leave town. You may find that they have linked their new problem to you and are either addicted to you or compulsively want to hurt you. Do you really want to risk that?

The fourth reason is metaphysical and what many people call "karmic." For those who hold strong to a belief about karma they will tell you that anything you do, good or bad, will come back to you. If, for any reason, you believe being good to people is better for you than the alternative then only use this knowledge for good.

Need I say more?

Qualifying Your Subject

To make sure the person you are working with is less likely to be one of those highly addictive personality types there are a few precautionary steps you can take.

Get to know them. Take your time. This will reveal if they have any existing behaviors of addiction. You can find out if their childhood was extremely difficult. Did they have parents who were unavailable, abusive or addicts themselves? Lastly, you can just ask them "do you think you have an addictive personality?"

If you have any doubt that they might be one of those addictive people then simply be kind and move on. Work with someone else to learn this skill.

If you are eager to test this material then it's best to work with healthy people, especially volunteers. Finding a volunteer can be as simple as asking, "what would like to be addicted to?" While many will say "no thanks," a few will consider their options. You could even suggest exercise or study.

www.BuildingYourCult.com

Building Your Cult

With all the warnings and precautions in place we can now move onto the qualities of the addictive pull.

The Addictive Pull

When a compelling pull is applied to influence someone they will tend to act with justification and reason because they are compelled by values, and those things that are important to them. The addictive pull, on the other hand, has less rationale and can be impossible to justify as reasonable. For this reason it is suggested that you use caution and compassion if you ever attempt to covertly apply it to someone.

All the better reason to first apply it to yourself and then apply it to volunteers who want a specific form of "addiction." This could be to working out, or healthy eating, or something similar.

To understand how the addictive pull is created you must remember that it is created by an emotional experience, and not by rational thought. As I have mentioned in previous publications we change by having experiences that are meaningful, not by reasoning things through.

This is what can make creating an addiction difficult for someone with limited experience in working with people. The reason why is that they must both be skilled at what they're doing and acutely aware of what's happening enough to keep their subject following their suggestions without suspicion.

It is like leading a bear into a trap...and you're the bait. You must be close enough to keep him following you *and* maintain enough distance to keep from getting caught. Like being chased by a bear, creating an addiction demands a great deal of effort and

Building Your Cult

attention.

There are plenty of places you can begin to create an addiction so why not begin with the compelling pull? By starting with the compelling pull as mentioned above you will create a deeper rapport with your subject and gain some highly valuable information that can be used later in the addictive pull process.

The next step is to elicit the mental and emotional state that I will call "gotta-have-it." For most people the gotta-have-it state is fleeting because we are able to push it aside and allow other more important things into our attention, but many of us are keenly aware of it when it hits us.

Perhaps you've passed a doughnut shop in your car and realized an unmistakable urge for one of their pastries...and turned around in order to get one. Or you might see a magazine headline at a store checkout counter that, for an moment, makes you feel as if you have to find out more. Whether you acted on the urge or not doesn't matter. For that instant you are in the gotta-have-it state.

Eliciting the gotta-have-it state is as simple as asking. Here are a couple of examples of what you could ask the subject.

"Have you ever thought of chocolate or some other food and realized you just gotta have it?"

"Have you ever had the experience of seeing a headline that made you want to learn more?"

"Can you remember a time when you drove to the store to buy something to eat because you wanted it so badly?"

You get the idea. The point is to engage the person in a

www.BuildingYourCult.com

conversation about that gotta-have-it feeling and engage them so thoroughly that they recreate that state momentarily within themselves.

Here I advise you do two things. First, encourage them and identify with them. This is to maintain both your rapport and the gotta-have-it state. At the same time you need to anchor the feeling.

Anchoring is mindlessly simple but often intimidating for anyone who isn't skilled at it. Anchoring consists of noticing when the subject is in the desired emotional state and then creating some sensory input – a touch, a sound, word or gesture – that can be linked to that state. When the sound, word, touch or gesture is repeated the subject experiences the state again as before. Anchoring can be considered an advanced form of dog training, except on humans.

While you receive a brief description of anchoring here you are encouraged to study more sources on the subject and always find situations to practice it.

Anchoring

The steps of anchoring can be broken down into four parts: eliciting the state, setting the anchor, testing the anchor, and firing the anchor.

Eliciting The State

Eliciting the state is what you were doing in the previous few paragraphs. It involves asking questions so that the subject begins to experience the thoughts and feelings of the state you want from them. In this case it's is a compulsive feeling, a strong "pull."

Building Your Cult

Setting The Anchor

Setting the anchor is done by creating a unique gesture, word or touch that will be used to remind them of the emotional state. This is done by being acutely aware of the subject when they begin to enter that state and at the moment their emotions begin to peak you set the anchor.

Testing The Anchor

Testing the anchor is an optional step, and when you have lots of experience with anchoring emotional states you'll simply know that that the anchor is "set." To test the anchor you would allow the subject to return to a neutral state, when the previous emotional state is not present, and see if by doing the anchor again (firing the anchor) the subject re-experiences the emotional state.

Firing The Anchor

Firing the anchor is done when the emotional state is strategically needed in order to get the result. In this case when you want the subject to feel the "pull" of addictive or compulsive desire you would fire the anchor.

While this may seem like a complicated process, in truth setting the anchor may take only seconds. Testing and firing the anchor may take just a few seconds more, but all of that comes with practice and experience.

Putting It All Together

How the whole process would work might go something like this. Let us assume you want someone you are attracted to call you each day during their lunch time.

First you gain rapport...this is vital. Next, elicit their

Building Your Cult

compelling pull for "people they are attracted to." In other words, you would ask, "what's important to you in someone you are **really** attracted to?," and continue with the questioning until you witness them reaching the emotions of the compelling pull.

Next you would change the subject and begin to ask what it's like when they have feelings of compulsions where they just **have to** do something because they feel compelled. As the state is elicited set the anchor for the state. Because you have rapport you can do this in a very fun and playful way. You can tell them, "let me show you something fun about how the mind works" and be very overt about it.

Once the anchor is set you can begin to describe the events that would fire off the anchor. *"Okay. Imagine now that you got the chance to take your lunch break. Could you imagine calling me (fire anchor)? Great! Could you see your next lunch break and feeling a desire to call me (fire anchor)? Great! And the lunch break after that you just **gotta call me** (fire anchor)...don't you?"*

This is most easily done in fun so that they feel as though it's a game or experiment. If you can do it with fun then you can go wild with it. You'll know it's working if they begin to smile and laugh. If they begin to laugh, all the better because you can use the laughter to make your suggestions stronger. *The more you laugh the more you want to call (fire anchor)? Don't you?"*

To do this well it does take an experimental trial and error attitude, a willingness to make mistakes and a bold and outrageous attitude. It will not always work perfectly all the time, but when it does work the results can be astounding.

The Propulsion System

Imagine your motivation being so focused that you go after

Building Your Cult

something with a single minded force of will. It's very likely you would eventually get whatever you were to focus on.

Imagine equally that you can create that same laser focused motivation in someone else, only now you also give them the goal and objective to focus on.

To understand the power of what you are creating imagine having two internal forces. It is the extreme version of the carrot and the stick with both carrot and stick being internal psychic forces that propel behavior. One force is a joy and elation for achieving a goal and the other force is a fear, dread and anxiety for not achieving it. Together these two forces act in the same way as squeezing a watermelon seed and the motivation shoots behaviors toward the goal.

This is referred to as a propulsion system. The difference between a propulsion system and an addiction is sometimes just a matter of semantics or labels.

To create a propulsion system you will need to use the tools we've already talked about, namely emotional state elicitation and anchoring.

For a propulsion system two states need to be elicited and anchored: one is a state of pleasure, excitement and joy and the other is a state of anxiety, guilt, shame and abject fear.

Once those states are anchored the pleasure anchor is fired and linked to an action or thought. The anxiety or fear anchor is fired and linked to **not** doing or thinking about the behavior.

A practical application of a propulsion system could be to create a drive towards making money. A person in a sales position could be made to feel joy, pleasure and excitement every time they generated a sale and they could be made to feel fear, guilt and anxiety if they are not working to make sales. The same could be made true for getting good grades and studying.

The same could be made true if you wanted someone to keep a secret. They would feel joy and success as long as the secret is kept but would fear the guilt, shame and loss if it slipped out.

With a more selfish and nefarious intent a man *could* create a propulsion system in a woman that compelled her to please him. I'll leave the rest to your imagination.

As with any process like this, a prerequisite to creating a propulsion system is rapport. Even better than rapport is getting the consent from the subject to complete the process, but it can be done covertly.

Step 1 – Build Rapport
Create a sense of rapport so that the other person willingly follows you or consents to follow your suggestions. Even better than that is an agreement on the type of propulsion system you are going to create.

Step 2 – Elicit The Joy/Excitement/Pleasure State And Anchor It
Ask questions that elicit the feelings of joy, pleasure and excitement. *"Can you recall a time when you felt incredible pleasure and excitement? Tell me about it."* Your rapport skills should allow you to notice when the subject is in the pleasure state and when to anchor it.

Step 3 – Elicit The Fear/Pain/Guilt State And Anchor It
Ask questions that contrast the joy and pleasure state in order to elicit the fear/pain/guilt state. *"Okay so you know what this joy feels*

Building Your Cult

like (pressing anchor). By contrast, what is the worst you've ever felt? Maybe it's fear or guilt or unbearable anxiety. Tell me about that."

Step 4 – Link The States To Behaviors And Thoughts
Ask the subject to rehearse the situation and their reactions with you. Here you would ask the subject to imagine themselves doing the behavior and experiencing the pleasure while you fire the pleasure/joy anchor. Be aware how fully they get into the state of pleasure.

Then you would create a contrasting situation where they are not doing the behavior and feeling anxious, guilty or fearful. At this point fire the fear/pain/guilt anchor. During your description make it clear that for them to feel any relief their only option is to do the behavior.

"Let's play a game. Go ahead and put yourself in the situation where you are now having the opportunity to X and, of course, you feel that pleasure and joy (fire pleasure anchor). That feels good!

*"Now you know how good that feels (fire anchor)...you can take a moment...a pause...and find yourself in that moment when you can't X...and you **really** want to. In fact, you can feel that discomfort (fire pain anchor) of not having it...not being able to X...and this feels (firing pain anchor) very uncomfortable."*

Step 5 – Future Pace The Results
Future pacing means to have the subject find specific moments in the future and placing that new response there in that moment. The key to future pacing is practicing it enough so the reaction happens every time they think about it without prompting.

"Now, imagine a time tonight when you have a chance to X and you

Building Your Cult

*feel that pleasure...don't you? (fire pleasure anchor)...but then you realize it's not going to happen (fire pain anchor) and...Oh No! You want to X so badly but...you can't. Then finally, **finally** you get that opportunity and ah...(fire pleasure anchor). That does feel good, doesn't it?"*

"Then tomorrow night, about the same time...you know where you are and what you are doing...and that opportunity to X again arises (fire pleasure anchor) and it feels so good.

"Then the night after (don't fire any anchors during this part to see if the reactions happen naturally) that you remember that wonderful pleasure, but you realize it's not going to happen...no matter what you do. That feels terrible. What do you do with that lingering in your mind...it won't go away."

Step 6 (optional) – Intensify By Linking The Results
This step is optional and adds a bit more complexity to the process. By adding this step you are linking the behavior more deeply to the subject's values. This step presumes you've taken the time elicit the compelling pull. All you have to do is link the positive behavior to the compelling pull.

"When I think of (name their compelling pull) the doing X really does fulfill it, doesn't it?"

Building Your Cult

Final Words

Whether you actually decide to start a cult is of no great concern to me.

If that is what you want to do then what you've learned here should give you a good start, and you **can** succeed at it. An another option would be to glean portions of what you've learned and apply it in your business or within your relationships. You could do both.

What I would most like you to do with this information is use it to improve yourself. You can be a refreshing change from the broken and neurotic cult leaders that we've both witnessed.

www.BuildingYourCult.com

Made in the USA
Charleston, SC
02 July 2010